STEVEN GERRARD

**World Cup
Heroes.**

STEVEN
GERRARD

Adam Cottier

JOHN BLAKE

Published by John Blake Publishing Ltd,
3 Bramber Court, 2 Bramber Road,
London W14 9PB, England

www.johnblakepublishing.co.uk

This edition published in paperback in 2010

ISBN: 978 1 84358 174 1

British Library Cataloguing-in-Publication Data:

A catalogue record for this book is available from the British Library.

Design by www.envydesign.co.uk

Printed in Great Britain by CPI Bookmarque, Croydon CR0 4TD

1 3 5 7 9 10 8 6 4 2

Papers used by John Blake Publishing are natural, recyclable products
made from wood grown in sustainable forests. The manufacturing processes
conform to the environmental regulations of the country of origin.

1

'I love Liverpool so much. This is my club. My heart is with Liverpool,' were the sincere words of Steven Gerrard following his decision to end weeks of torment for Liverpool fans and sign a lucrative new contract with his hometown club in July 2005. Less than two months earlier, the inspirational captain, adored by so many, had lifted the European Cup after leading his side to the most unbelievable footballing comeback of all time. However, in the weeks to come, all the joy and jubilation from that incredible night in Istanbul were overshadowed by an episode in Gerrard's career that saw his lifelong ties to Liverpool FC come perilously close to being severed forever.

The arrival of Russian billionaire Roman Abramovich at Chelsea in 2004 signalled a frenzy of multi-million-pound transfer activity. Almost inevitably, they courted the Liverpool captain. In 2004, Gerrard turned them down, deciding instead to remain with his beloved, albeit underachieving, team. And his desire for silverware duly ended, with an unlikely European Cup winners' medal. However, Liverpool still failed to gain any ground in their bid for an elusive Premiership title. Gerrard was forced to think long and hard about leaving Anfield, knowing that, if he did so, he would break the hearts of the fans he had made so happy.

'How could I leave after this?' the Liverpool captain had said after leading his hometown club to glory on the biggest stage possible.

The answer was simple: he would leave if Liverpool wanted the immeasurable amount of money that Chelsea were willing to pay for him.

Liverpool fans feared the worst as Gerrard holidayed in Portugal with his girlfriend and his baby daughter, amid rumours that the Reds were not about to offer him a new contract. The club dawdled, so much so that Gerrard came to the point where he believed the club he loved so dearly no longer wanted him. Before lifting the European Cup, he had warned Liverpool that, as much as it would hurt him, he would seek a transfer should the club failed to meet his expectations. However, the magic of that triumph had alleviated any doubt as to whether Anfield was the place where he could realise his childhood dreams.

Gerrard's ongoing contract riddle was not the only concern Liverpool had after winning the Champions League. They were told that their victory would not warrant their automatic re-entry into the competition and that they would only feature in the UEFA Cup, as they had finished outside of the Champions League qualifying positions in the Premiership. To the club's relief, however,

UEFA decided to allow them back in, but only if they could overcome three allotted rounds of qualifying, which would begin in mid-July. That meant that Liverpool had to return to pre-season training early, barely six weeks after the previous season had ended. With increasing doubt surrounding Gerrard's situation, Liverpool fans held their breath as their side began preparations for their first qualifying match.

'The ball's in Liverpool's court now,' said Gerrard, frustrated by the breakdown in communication on the club's part. 'Of course, I want to stay at Liverpool. We haven't spoken about a new contract yet, so I don't know how long the talks will go on for. The sooner we get under way the better, because I want my future sorted out before the season starts.'

Real Madrid became the Fleet Street favourite to land the talismanic maestro, closely followed by Chelsea. A move to Spain to join David Beckham and Michael Owen looked increasingly likely, until Real decided to bolster their star-studded staff with little-known Uruguayan midfielder Pablo Garcia, a player said to possess the same dynamic and industrial abilities of Gerrard. Garcia's arrival at the Bernabeu suggested that Real had lost patience with Liverpool.

Chelsea launched a sizeable bid amid newspaper rumours of a tarnished relationship between Gerrard and his manager, Rafa Benitez. The Champions League final seemed light years away. Benitez himself, desperate to preserve Liverpool's future, issued an impassioned plea for Gerrard to remain on Merseyside. It had been thought that, following Gerrard's unerring post-match declaration in

Istanbul and Benitez's insistence that he wanted to build his team around his inspirational captain, contract negotiations were just a formality. However, Gerrard and his agent, Struan Marshall, had found Liverpool's hesitancy intolerable. The English midfielder had become convinced that he was unwanted by his employers. Then, on Monday, 4 July 2005, it was announced that Gerrard and his advisers had called a halt to contract discussions. The Liverpool heart had stopped beating.

'The last six weeks have been the toughest of my life and it's the hardest decision I have ever had to make,' said Gerrard. 'I fully intended to sign a new contract after the Champions League final, but the events of the last five or six weeks have changed all that. I have too much respect for the club to get involved in a slanging match.'

There seemed to be no way back as Chelsea waded in for the kill. They launched a staggering £32 million bid that same July evening. Benitez and Rick Parry, the Liverpool chief executive at the time, held an emergency meeting with Gerrard and his agent in the hope of reviving contract discussions. Despite their willingness to offer a new deal worth more than £90,000 a week, the discussions ended with Anfield officials finally conceding that they had lost the battle. An acrimonious separation loomed large.

The Reds' only hope of keeping Gerrard rested with the player himself. He spent hours mulling over his future and agonising over his decision on Liverpool's contract offer. He had confided in friends that he desperately wanted to stay at Anfield, but that he was concerned that the club wouldn't be strong enough to compete for honours in the forthcoming season. Chelsea offered an appealing alternative.

Liverpool fans gathered outside Anfield, some of them even burning shirts to express their disgust at Gerrard's apparent disloyalty. Meanwhile, Chelsea's bid was rejected as a sense of urgency encroached on Liverpool's hierarchy to resolve the matter swiftly. The thought of Gerrard returning to Anfield the following season in a blue shirt was, as the *Liverpool Echo* put it, 'too hideous to contemplate'.

Gerrard had been talked out of signing for Chelsea in the summer of 2004 by his father Paul. Although he would have doubled his £60,000-a-week wages, Paul reportedly told his son that if he left Liverpool then life would become intolerable for the family. The same plea worked again.

On the morning of Wednesday, 6 July, the talk was of Gerrard's imminent transfer to Chelsea. However, by lunchtime, it became very clear that the Liverpool captain had made an incredible U-turn to remain with the European champions.

'I had the whole of yesterday to think about my decision and what I was doing. I turned off my phone and my television and went through it all in my head again,' revealed Gerrard. 'I just couldn't leave the club I love.'

In the aftermath, Liverpool and Gerrard himself admitted that they had made mistakes. The 25-year-old had been convinced that Benitez had secretly wanted to sell him and that that was the only reason why contract negotiations had gone on for so long. Gerrard pleaded for forgiveness for his part in the saga.

'In my heart, this is my club. I want to help bring success here for them and, for their sake and my own, I never want to go through this again. The last five or six weeks were the hardest of my life, because I wrongly believed the club didn't want me... Now I know how much the club want me... I've only one medal left to win at Liverpool and that's the Premiership. That's what I want more than anything and Liverpool is the only place where I've ever wanted to win it.'

The romance was back on and both parties got the chance to renew their vows as Liverpool faced Wrexham in a pre-season game at the Racecourse Ground. It was hardly St Paul's Cathedral, or even Istanbul's Ataturk Stadium for that matter, but it would do for now, as Liverpool put their troubles behind them and embarked on a new season.

2

The city of Liverpool will never forget 1980. It was the year in which legendary Beatle John Lennon met his untimely death. Yet it was also the year that a small community of Merseyside welcomed a new arrival – a person who would one day realise the same kind of iconic status that Lennon had embraced on Merseyside.

Steven George Gerrard was born on Friday, 30 May 1980 at Whiston Hospital in the borough of Knowsley, on the eastern outskirts of Liverpool, the second son of Paul Gerrard and his wife Julie. There was a champion feeling in the Liverpool-mad Gerrard family. The Reds, led by Bob Paisley, had just been crowned title winners in England for the twelfth time.

Although Everton were successful in the 1980s – the most successful they have ever been – the Reds were domestically dominant throughout the decade. And it was their European Cup success of 1984 that probably swung Gerrard in the red direction, igniting a love affair that would last a lifetime. The Rome final fell on what was his fourth birthday, and how his infant eyes must have sparkled that night as Graeme Souness inspired the Reds to beat Roma on penalties and lift the giant trophy.

It was on the playing fields of the Bluebell estate in the football-mad suburb of Huyton that Gerrard fully realised his love for the game. Untamed dreams of playing for his hometown club, winning trophies and starring in Merseyside derbies were played out avidly every day. And there could not have been a greater influence on any young aspiring footballer than Liverpool's all-conquering side of the time. As the likes of Ronnie Whelan, Steve McMahon and John Barnes graced Anfield in the late 1980s, Gerrard was imitating them just a few miles away on the streets of the Liverpool council estate he lived on.

'I grew up on a council estate and I loved every minute of it,' Gerrard told the *Sunday Times*. 'I used to hang around lads who were two or three years older than me, because my brother, Paul, is that age. They were the ones who always seemed to be playing football and I played with them... We had a car park outside our house and we put a goal up at one end of it and played every second we could. It was great growing up with my mates there, but a lot of them are unemployed now, so I do think about what I might have been doing without football.'

Football in Liverpool in the 1980s was an adhesive bond, helped by the success of both the top clubs on Merseyside – it served a solid purpose in a society that might otherwise have been blighted by crime and poverty. Talents were nurtured and spotted early. Children focused solely on improving. Despite their impoverished roots, children would steer clear of crime thanks to football. It is the reason why so many young players who grew up at the same time in Liverpool have made it as footballers on a grand scale.

Gerrard's earliest Anfield memory was when Liverpool played Coventry in a League Cup fourth-round replay on 26 November 1986. Anfield was only half-full that night, but it didn't stop Gerrard from cherishing such a special moment. A crowd of just over 19,000 accompanied him in watching Liverpool progress, courtesy of a 3–1 victory. Midfielder Jan Molby, that master of the pass, scored a hat-trick of penalties. The inspiration was there for Gerrard to seize upon.

Liverpool won the league in 1987, and once again in 1988, before they were spectacularly humbled by Wimbledon in the FA Cup final later that same year. In 1989, tragedy struck at Hillsborough at the FA Cup semi-final tie between Liverpool and Nottingham Forest, before Liverpool went on to win in the final against Everton just over a month later. But in the league Michael Thomas's extraordinary late winner at Anfield had handed Arsenal the title at Liverpool's expense. That moment sparked a decade of relative anonymity by Kop standards, with only their 1992 FA Cup final victory and a League Cup final victory in 1995 to show for it. While taking a firm interest in Liverpool's trials and tribulations, Gerrard also watched and admired the midfield heroics of England's talisman Paul Gascoigne – the player who he would go on to emulate on the international stage some ten years later.

Gerrard's first school was St Michael's Primary School in Huyton, now called Huyton-with-Roby Primary. Back then, the other boys towered over him, but his fragile appearance was deceptive. When Gerrard was in possession of a ball on the school's bumpy playing fields, his footballing abilities became instantly obvious – he looked more able than players twice his age.

'I just couldn't believe he was so good, because he was one of the smallest boys in the class,' Mike Tilling, Gerrard's tutor of the time, told the *Liverpool Echo*. 'I started him off as a striker and it honestly seemed as if he had been playing for years – he was so good with the ball at his feet.'

Gerrard played for his primary-school football team from the moment he moved into year three. Most children would not even be considered until year six. He had an extraordinarily precocious talent. What he lacked in mass, he more than made up for in character and strength. Even in class, away from a football, Gerrard was the cream of the crop.

'We used to run a little business in the class,' explains Tilling. 'It was owned by the children and Steven would always win hands down when we voted for who the manager would be.'

No matter how comfortable Gerrard was in the classroom, his outstanding talent was football. In 1990, he won his first piece of silverware, the Huyton Under-11s Schools' League Title.

When Tilling left the school to take up a new teaching post elsewhere, all the children in his class signed a card to say thank you. Gerrard wrote his name in huge letters across the middle of the page. Perhaps that served as a symbol of what he was going to become – a midfield giant and the centrepiece of a team. What it definitely symbolised was an amiable young man's gratitude for the first person that had helped him outside of his family. It was the first measure of a true champion schoolboy.

While at St Michael's, Gerrard was invited by George Hughes to play for Sunday-league side Whiston Juniors.

'Even as a nipper Steven was streets ahead of all the other lads,' Hughes said. 'We knew he was special straight away. He could take the opposition on by himself – he was that good.'

Hughes was so impressed with Gerrard's abilities that he alerted friends at the Liverpool School of Excellence, run by Reds legend Steve Heighway. A guided tour of Anfield, followed by a successful trial, propelled the eight-year-old into the cradle of the Liverpool Football Club. 1988 may have seen Liverpool reduced to tears by Wimbledon, but it was also the year that a future European Cup winner began his Anfield association. Gerrard trained twice a week there up until the age of 16, when he signed professional forms. While he was there, he developed a blossoming friendship with Michael Owen, despite the fact that the pair had very different domestic backgrounds.

Gerrard's progress in his early teenage years was hampered by Osgood-Schlatter's disease, a bone condition that meant that he was seldom fit for more than a week at a time. Had he been any less motivated, then the growing pains he had to endure would almost certainly have ended his footballing dreams, but he has always been a fighter and a winner – especially in the face of adversity.

Whereas Owen is estimated to have played around 90 games in two seasons at Under-13 and Under-14 level with

Liverpool, Gerrard managed barely 30 outings. Such infrequency meant that he missed out on selection for the national football school at Lilleshall in Shropshire, where Owen went to have his talents primed for success. Jamie Carragher also made it to the national football school. The legacy of that traumatic period in Gerrard's life lived on. Even when his Liverpool career was taking off a few years later, he was still visiting an osteopath in Paris on a regular basis.

Wrapped in cotton wool by Liverpool, Gerrard pulled through. Such was his ability at the age of 13, he was picked a year early for the Liverpool schoolboys' team. He impressed his coaches with his commitment and willingness. One such coach was Tim Johnson. 'I remember the first round of the English Trophy, which was the schoolboys' equivalent of the FA Cup,' Johnson told the *Liverpool Echo*. 'Steven scored the winner against West Lancashire and it was at the time of Jurgen Klinsmann, so when he scored he dived into the corner on his stomach. There was a lot of tut-tutting on the sidelines, but he really played his heart out for Liverpool schoolboys.'

Gerrard and Owen were the cornerstone of their schoolboy side. Back then the pair were very similar in terms of physical stature and their coaches were eager to nurture their abilities. In one instance, Gerrard and Owen were the only two Under-14 players taken on an Under-18 tour of Spain – not to play, but to learn. It benefited them greatly.

Three years after joining the Liverpool School of Excellence, Gerrard switched primary school for secondary, when he made the move to the Cardinal Heenan

Roman Catholic School in West Derby. It was there that his sporting skills bore even more fruit.

Gerrard was an expert in athletics: a natural at throwing the javelin and also the shot-put. He was also the best in his age group at the 400 metres and he was the school's tennis champion for four years.

But football was his one true love. He scored a hat-trick in his first game for Cardinal Heenan in an 8–0 win over Savio High, the school that Carragher attended. Better things were to follow. At the end of his first year, Gerrard donned the captain's armband for the Merseyside Under-11s Cup final. Playing against the renowned Bluecoat High School, Cardinal Heenan found themselves 3–0 down at half-time. Half the Cardinal Heenan side were already resigned to losing, but not Gerrard – he was different to his team-mates; an inspirational leader even then.

Gerrard, as he would go on to do against AC Milan, proceeded to pull a goal back early in the second half. He went on to score again and, before he knew it, his side had won 4–3. It was a foretaste of that memorable night in Istanbul 14 years later, though there were no penalties this time. It was Captain Fantastic in the making.

Steve Monaghan, his coach and head of year at Cardinal Heenan, remembers that afternoon with great fondness. 'Steven brought the team all back with him that day and you could see that something was building,' Monaghan told the *Liverpool Echo*. 'It was typical of his attitude. Even as a young lad he was good at rallying his team; he led by example and had that tremendous commitment. He always had the ability to say, "No, we're not beaten here."'

Gerrard was not only a role model to his fellow pupils on the sports field; according to Monaghan, he was a model class-member. 'He was a little angel-faced blonde. But he was a good pupil, there was never a discipline problem and, although his exams did take second place later on, he didn't give up like some lads do, thinking he was definitely going to make it as a footballer.'

Gerrard's love and hunger for football and, perhaps more evidently, his desire to win was not reserved for the school playing fields. He often accompanied his father, who he still calls his greatest influence, to watch school matches all over Merseyside. More often than not, the team Gerrard wanted to see were Cardinal Heenan's next opponents. After meticulously examining his future opponents' strengths and weaknesses, Gerrard would return to his teacher's office with a detailed report on the team they were about to face. It is no surprise, then, that Gerrard remained unbeaten as captain of his school football team for three years. His final act for Cardinal Heenan was to lift the Royal Mail Trophy in his last game as captain before he joined the Liverpool academy. He left a lasting legacy on all those who had the opportunity to be alongside him on and off the pitch.

'Steven was different class,' one of Gerrard's former school-mates, Ben Chadwick, told the press. 'He could do everything. I don't think I ever saw him lose a tackle and his passing was unbelievable. If he didn't know you, he was quiet and shy, but, once you gained his confidence, he was a typical Scouser with a great sense of humour.'

To this day, Gerrard has never forgotten his modest football roots and he remains ever proud of them. He regularly visits Cardinal Heenan school and has opened its sports centre and appeared at prize-giving presentations. It was on those rough edges of Liverpool that Gerrard's true talent came to the fore and he remains eternally grateful to those who taught him and encouraged him to follow his dreams.

3

Gerrard signed professional forms at Anfield upon leaving Cardinal Heenan High School shortly after his 16th birthday. It was 1996, and the majority of his friends from Huyton were leaving school to become electricians, plumbers or call-centre workers; some even ended up on the dole. However, the school-leaver with a true, sparkling ability moved a giant step closer to realising his childhood dream under the wing of Liverpool legend Steve Heighway. Another teenager with an abundance of talent, Michael Owen, also graduated to the youth-training scheme alongside Gerrard. The pair were the only two players to be kept on Liverpool's books. In the capable hands of the former Reds hero, both Gerrard and Owen progressed at an astonishing rate.

As a 16-year-old, Gerrard still had the same slender, injury-prone frame that had hampered him during his school days. Fearing a wasted talent, Mother Nature decided that things needed to change. In just over a year,

Gerrard went from being a pint-sized 5ft 4in nipper to being a 6ft 1in midfield maestro. His size and proportion had always been a worry for his coaches in terms of whether or not he could make it on to the big stage. The transformation left them stunned.

'Young Stevie had the most amazing growth spurt,' recalled Tim Johnson, Liverpool schoolboys' coach. 'I was at the academy some 18 months after he had finished playing for me and this colossus appeared in the doorway of the sports hall. I just couldn't believe my eyes. I couldn't take it in that it was the same Stevie Gerrard. The Bambi that had left me had turned into a bison.'

In that year or so of transformation, Gerrard's near-telepathic on-the-field relationship with Owen also grew stronger. He often played at right-back during his initiation and it was from that position that his trademark long passing and extraordinary vision came to fruition, helping Owen bag the goals that propelled the prolific striker into the first team. Disciplined and refined, together the pair encroached on Liverpool's failing senior side that had been bereft of major silverware for almost a decade. It was Owen who made it there first, partly aided by the fact that he had played for England at schoolboy level whereas Gerrard had not.

Owen made his first-team debut as a second-half replacement for Patrik Berger in Liverpool's away defeat to Wimbledon on 7 May 1997. Fourteen minutes into his professional career, the 17-year-old took Stig Inge Bjornebye's pass in his stride and guided home his first Liverpool goal. In the season that followed, Owen rose to prominence as Liverpool's main marksman, taking that particular mantle away from the club's original 1990s protégé Robbie Fowler. At the 1998 World Cup, Owen announced himself to the world with an incredible goal in England's second-round tie against Argentina.

In the meantime, Gerrard waited patiently for his chance. Owen had made a telling impression with his electric pace and exceptional eye for goal; it wasn't as easy for Gerrard, but a managerial change at Anfield proved decisive.

Gérard Houllier's arrival at the club in July 1998, initially to become joint-manager alongside Roy Evans, brought fresh hope to the long-suffering fans of Liverpool and no doubt to the eager young stars of the academy. The Reds had finished third in the Premiership in the previous season, but, having witnessed Arsene Wenger's success in leading Arsenal to their Double triumph of that year, they set about their own French revolution – believing that Houllier would have the same effect.

The unique double act led Liverpool into the new season with expectations rocketing. Robbie Fowler was in the midst of a long injury lay-off, so the onus was on Owen to make an even bigger impression. He started well, hitting the winner as Houllier's new charges came from behind to beat Southampton at the Dell on the opening day of the 1998/99 season.

The return of Jamie Redknapp from a cartilage problem that had ruled him out of the 1998 World Cup was hailed by Houllier as the key ingredient in Liverpool's drive for success. After a devastating Owen hat-trick away at Newcastle and a 2–0 defeat of Coventry, the Reds were on top of the table. But an away defeat at West Ham followed, and cracks in an obscure managerial marriage began to show.

By early November, having won just one game in eight, Liverpool were fast becoming mid-table nonentities. The fireworks exploded on Evans's 33-year Anfield residence when a home defeat to Spurs prematurely ended the Reds' challenge in the League Cup on 10 November 1998. Houllier was left in sole charge of arresting an alarming decline that seemed to be spiralling out of control.

Houllier, who had made his name as technical director with the renowned French youth academy, decided it was time to look to Liverpool's own youth ranks to find an answer to his troubles. Houllier was no stranger to picking out young talent from a crowd of hopefuls. And he was no stranger to Merseyside either, having started his working life there in the 1960s as a teacher. With big-money transfers ruled out, Houllier had to use his old skills again to find the most talented pupils in his new school.

In the weeks leading up to Liverpool's UEFA Cup third-round tie against Celta Vigo, Houllier decided to take in some Under-19 games at Melwood in search of a solution. And that was when he first set eyes on Gerrard.

'I could see very quickly that he was something special, that he was a special talent. It was a funny situation, really, because he was thought to be too young at the time and I was supposed to be looking at other players, but he was the player I saw. I knew straight away that he was the one I wanted. He was a different class.'

Three days after Robbie Fowler announced his return

from injury with a sensational hat-trick as Liverpool thumped Aston Villa at Villa Park, the Reds headed for Spain for their UEFA Cup tie in confident mood, having seen off another Spanish outfit, Valencia, in the previous round of the competition. An unfamiliar face sat among Liverpool's tracksuit-clad warriors bound for Europe. Gerrard, at just 18 years old, had been invited to accompany the senior squad for the first time.

Although he didn't feature in Liverpool's 3–1 defeat to Celta Vigo, it was a valuable tutorial for Gerrard as he rubbed shoulders with his future team-mates for the first time. The following Sunday, as Liverpool prepared to entertain struggling Blackburn Rovers, Gerrard – having shown Houllier that he was ready for his big moment – was named among the Reds' substitutes. In the 90th minute of that match, which Liverpool won 2–0, he tore off his tracksuit and ran on to the Anfield turf for the very first time as a direct replacement for Norwegian right-back Vegard Heggem. The new kid on the block could barely catch his breath as the full-time whistle resonated around Anfield, but he was at the beginning of a breathtaking Liverpool career.

Such was Houllier's faith in Gerrard that he didn't wait for an easy game to hand him his full debut. Instead, he selected him to play against Tottenham Hotspur at White Hart Lane, with the onerous responsibility of marking David Ginola, the flamboyant Frenchman blessed with sublime skills.

It turned out to be an experience that Gerrard did not enjoy. Ginola handed him a torturous Premiership baptism and he was substituted in the second half. 'I remember travelling home thinking, It's not my game, this. I'm getting out of it,' he later recalled. But Houllier believed he had the character to bounce back.

The next game was the UEFA Cup third-round second leg tie with Celta Vigo at Anfield. Gerrard took his place in a youthful Liverpool line-up that included fellow academy graduates David Thompson, Jamie Carragher, Michael Owen and, coming on as substitute, Danny Murphy. Even if Liverpool's frailties were exposed that night as the Spanish side progressed with a 1–0 victory, Gerrard announced himself to the Kop with an assured and exemplary performance, one that was beyond his years.

During his debut season, Gerrard made 12 appearances in the first team – making four starts and featuring eight times as a substitute – while Liverpool limped to a seventh-place finish in the Premiership. He was even invited to experience life with Kevin Keegan's England squad preparing for their European Championship qualifier against Poland in March 1999. Despite that honour, undoubtedly the highlight for him that season came in his first-ever Merseyside derby a month later.

With Liverpool leading 3–2 inside a packed Anfield, Gerrard, playing at right-back having come on as a 71st-minute substitute, showed his fighting, never-say-die attitude to react tremendously and repel a goal-bound shot from Everton's Danny Cadamarteri right on the goal-line. It effectively won Liverpool fans the Merseyside bragging rights for that year and also earned Gerrard a rousing ovation from the Kop.

But Liverpool had endured another wretched season by their own high standards; they didn't even qualify for

Europe. At least they seemed to have a bright future – led by a local teenager who had grown from being a mere pint-sized prospect into a potential Anfield stalwart. For Liverpool and Gerrard, the only way was up.

4

The 1999/2000 season saw Gerrard make his outright indelible mark on the Liverpool senior side. Gérard Houllier began his first full season in sole charge, getting rid of the likes of David James, Paul Ince and Steve McManaman and spending £21 million on new talent. Jamie Redknapp was handed the captain's armband as the Reds began the Houllier era for real.

Dietmar Hamann's arrival seemed set to scupper Gerrard's dream of moving into a central midfield role and the youngster's prospects looked bleaker when he wasn't even named among the substitutes as Liverpool opened the new campaign with a 2–1 victory at Sheffield Wednesday. However, only 24 minutes into that game, Hamann had to be withdrawn, suffering from ankle-ligament damage. The door was open, and Owen for one knew who should walk through it.

'Steve will be our star man this season,' Owen had exclaimed before the start of the season. 'I am not just saying that because we are good friends – he is brilliant.'

Sure enough, Gerrard was called up to partner Redknapp in midfield against newly promoted Watford, who proceeded to stun the Kop with an unlikely 1–0 victory. With the Reds lacking bite in midfield, Gerrard's future in the first team looked to be in jeopardy when he was substituted midway through the second half. David Thompson, who replaced him, and Danny Murphy, were both vying for that particular position.

Gerrard was in and out, still struggling to stamp his name on the midfield berth, and he didn't help his cause when Liverpool met Everton at Anfield on 28 September 1999. Hamann made his comeback from injury and replaced Gerrard in Liverpool's starting XI, but this particular Merseyside derby was war – not even the substitutes were safe from the firing line of bad temper that ensued that evening. Kevin Campbell put Everton ahead inside the first five minutes. Then, midway through the second half, Everton's young forward Francis Jeffers clashed with Sander Westerveld, the Liverpool goalkeeper. The pair exchanged slaps and Westerveld grabbed Jeffers by the neck, resulting in a red card for both players from referee Mike Riley.

Liverpool's ignominy was compounded as defender Steve Staunton was forced to take the gloves, with the three allowed substitutions having already been made. But it didn't end there. Liverpool pressed forward in vain, searching for an equaliser. It never came and, to make matters worse, Gerrard, who had entered the fray as a 64th-minute substitute for Robbie Fowler, was sent off for a waist-high, two-footed lunge on Kevin Campbell.

A three-match suspension duly followed, and Houllier

made his feelings known by not speaking to Gerrard for a week. When he returned from suspension, Gerrard was an unused substitute in Liverpool's 1–0 victory over West Ham at Anfield. Then he was left out of the squad completely while Liverpool cantered to a 3–1 victory over Bradford. It was obvious that he had his work cut out if he wanted to force his way back into Houllier's good books.

An injury to club captain Jamie Redknapp came as a blessing in disguise for Gerrard. Redknapp's persistent knee problem saw him ruled out for three months with cartilage damage. Gerrard slotted into his desired central midfield position, playing behind Hamann in a 1–0 away defeat to West Ham. 'A solid if unspectacular look' was how the *Observer* described Liverpool's midfield pairing.

But Houllier had announced that he wanted to 'keep a Liverpool heart beating' within the club, and, with Steven Gerrard, David Thompson and Danny Murphy starting to make the grade in the first team alongside previous graduates Jamie Carragher and Michael Owen, there was at least some basis for hope and local pride among the Kopites.

Sheffield Wednesday at home, Sunday, 5 December 1999, is a game and a day that will be etched on Steven Gerrard's memory forever. Live on Sky Sports, Liverpool's credentials were thrust back into the public spotlight. Of the 14 players that Houllier employed that afternoon, seven had come through the youth ranks at Anfield, including the new wave of Owen, Thompson, Dominic Matteo and Gerrard, who all began the match. The 42,517 spectators present were treated to a dazzling display of precocious talent.

With Liverpool leading 2–1, the moment came for Gerrard's first senior goal for the club. With purpose and poise, the 19-year-old gathered the ball 40 yards from goal and burst forward. He weaved his way around the close attention of Brazilian stalwart Emerson Thome and former England defender Des Walker before slotting a cool, right-footed shot wide of Kevin Pressman and into the net. The Kop erupted in sincere admiration of a remarkable goal.

Liverpool came crashing back to earth with a bump when they broke into the new millennium with a 1–0 defeat at Tottenham, followed by a shock exit from the FA Cup against First Division Blackburn Rovers at Anfield. If Liverpool needed a reminder that Gérard Houllier was some way short of having a trophy-winning squad, it came when Nathan Blake sealed a shock 1–0 victory for the Lancashire side four minutes from time.

Gerrard had been employed at right-back again, as Houllier continued to shuffle his pack, but he returned to central midfield alongside David Thompson in a hard-fought 3–2 victory at Watford, which began a 13-match unbeaten run that propelled Liverpool to the brink of European qualification.

Owen's injury problems saw him ruled out until March, joining Redknapp and Fowler on the Anfield treatment table. For most of Liverpool's young stars forced to step into the breach, it was make or break time. The run-in to the end of the season saw Gerrard earn more praise, one of his keenest admirers being the England manager preparing for a major tournament.

'I've watched Gerrard a few times now and I've seen him do an excellent job,' Kevin Keegan told the *Mail on*

Sunday. 'If he continues in that vein and stays fit, I'll fetch him in.'

Gerrard came face to face with a childhood idol when Middlesbrough visited Anfield in late January. In the Boro midfield that day was one Paul Gascoigne.

'I used to try and model myself on Gazza, but it never worked,' Gerrard told the *Independent*. 'He was so exciting to watch; you never knew what to expect from him. I liked the way he could go past people and score goals... I tried to nutmeg him in the game. It never came off and he gave me a slap on the back of the head and told me to start behaving.'

Gerrard was clearly beginning to enjoy his flourishing Liverpool career and the chance of playing against his idols.

'It's a nice time for a young lad to come in at Liverpool with the team doing so well. We are in a Champions League qualifying position and we hope to stay ahead of Chelsea and Arsenal. I know how much European football means to Liverpool fans and maybe, in three or four years, we could win a European medal. I think we are still behind Manchester United and Arsenal, but we are gradually improving as a team.'

Newspapers began to speculate on whether Gerrard, having performed so remarkably for Liverpool since the turn of the year, would be included in Keegan's squad for a friendly against Argentina at Wembley.

'People are now asking the question "Are you ready for England?" My answer is that any footballer should be confident in his own ability and I say, "Why shouldn't I play for the England team?" I've heard I'm going to be named if I'm fit and, if the call does come, I'll be excited.

Then I'll just go and do what I've been doing for Liverpool all season. I'm relaxed about the England thing, but my mum and dad and my older brother Paul are a bit anxious.'

On Thursday, 17 February 2000, Gerrard, despite a groin injury, was named in the England senior squad for the first time in his career. Leeds midfielder Lee Bowyer and West Ham's Frank Lampard had been overlooked in favour of the Liverpool man, and pundits quickly jumped on the bandwagon of admiration for the 19-year-old Reds star. Chris Kamara, the former Bradford manager and Sky television pundit, likened Gerrard to former England midfield hero Bryan Robson. With his fierce tackling and unshakeable will to win, he certainly bore comparison.

'Whenever I have watched him – or whenever I have read a report on him – he has been outstanding,' said Keegan. 'His versatility excites me; you can ask him to do any number of jobs. In a squad of 22, there is room for that. I also love the way he passes a ball – he can play one-twos and hit it 30 or 40 yards. He has a great future.'

Gerrard joined up with his new team-mates at England's Bisham Abbey headquarters, still hoping to shake off his groin problem. Sadly, the game came too soon for him, and England earned a creditable goalless draw against Argentina at Wembley without his services.

The injury had become a set-back in Gerrard's campaign to be an Anfield regular. Houllier signed Emile Heskey from Leicester for £11 million to bolster his striking options and the new man was an instant hit, winning a penalty minutes into his debut – a 1–1 draw with Sunderland at Anfield. Gerrard joined Heskey back in

Liverpool's starting XI, but struggled to make an impact and was replaced at half-time by Danny Murphy.

With Jamie Redknapp on the brink of a return from injury, Gerrard was suddenly struggling for a guaranteed place once more. A goalless draw at home to Aston Villa saw him substituted for Redknapp 12 minutes from the end. With only 10 games remaining, the pressure was on Liverpool to secure a place in the Champions League.

Gerrard returned to central midfield for a crucial 2–0 win at Derby County. He was looking more confident by the game, more influential and more likely to crown his first full season with an England cap. With a Champions League place now within Liverpool's reach, Newcastle United came to Anfield looking to halt the Reds' charge. Gerrard was his orchestrating self again – providing a precision pass for Titi Camara to put Liverpool ahead early in the second half. But Alan Shearer headed an equaliser and Liverpool were left requiring new impetus. That renewed energy came in the shape of fit-again Jamie Redknapp, who came off the bench to replace Gerrard, and promptly headed Liverpool's winning goal.

The luckless Anfield captain then injured an ankle in a midweek reserve game and his comeback was put on hold again. And Gerrard was at his gallant best once more as Liverpool crushed Coventry 3–0 at Highfield Road. Owen was also at his lethal best, scoring a first-half double before Heskey scored his first Liverpool goal to crown a fine display. Gerrard was instrumental in both of Owen's goals, before being replaced by Danny Murphy with 20 minutes remaining, having worked himself into the ground. Houllier was using his managerial expertise to ensure that the youngster did not suffer a burnout in the infancy of his Liverpool career. Gerrard was rested as Liverpool moved up to second in the Premiership with a 2–0 home win over Spurs.

Having recharged his batteries, he was back alongside Hamann in the heart of the Liverpool midfield as the Reds marked the 11th anniversary of the Hillsborough tragedy with an away win at Wimbledon. Heskey's brace earned Houllier's men a 2–1 victory – they turned out to be Liverpool's last goals of the season with five games still remaining.

Gerrard picked up another groin injury and he was absent as Liverpool saw their Champions League hopes all but evaporate with a goalless draw in their last home game of the season against Southampton. He did return to see out the season, a 1–0 defeat away at Bradford that confirmed a season that had promised much.

In all, Gerrard made 28 appearances, scoring one goal and earning a place on the shortlist for the PFA Young Player of the Year award. Liverpool finished fourth, some 24 points behind champions Manchester United. They also finished just two points adrift of a Champions League place. UEFA Cup qualification was all Liverpool had to show from a season of renewed optimism, direction and purpose. However, Gérard Houllier's reign was slowly but surely heading in the direction of success.

5

Gerrard had to be quick in casting aside Liverpool's disappointment at not qualifying for the Champions League. His whirlwind breakthrough season had seen him mature into the kind of versatile and robust footballer that any international manager would be glad to have on board – including Kevin Keegan.

On 29 March 2000, Gerrard had won his fourth and final cap for England Under-21s, in a European Under-21 Championship qualifying play-off with Yugoslavia in Barcelona. The game was supposed to have been played over two legs later in the year, but war in Kosovo, and perhaps fate, determined that a neutral venue would host the play-off and England's young stars would get a chance to impress Keegan.

David Batty, the Leeds United midfielder, looked set to be ruled out of the summer tournament due to continuing injury problems, and Jamie Redknapp was also losing his battle for fitness. Gerrard was the most likely of the Under-

21s to step up and help solve one of Keegan's main problems. And his dazzling performance against Yugoslavia proved that his young legs were ready. He played as a holding midfielder in front of a three-man defence. Versatile and mobile, his tackling was both timely and decisive: his vision and passing devastatingly accurate.

In the 63rd minute, he delivered a cross-field pass for Derby's Seth Johnson who, in turn, set up Lee Hendrie to score England's third goal in a 3–0 victory. The Liverpool midfielder was left stunned by his own fine form.

'Really, England is a dream – something that at the start of the season I would never have even dared think about,' he said. 'I never expected to come this far so soon. But now that I have set such high standards, I just want to keep it going. I am desperate to get in the final 22 for the European Championships.'

Keegan had undoubtedly already made up his mind. Gerrard was just so energetic and so fresh. There wasn't a better English ball-winning midfielder around at the time.

'I have probably watched Steven Gerrard more than any other player this season,' Keegan exclaimed on his return from Barcelona. 'He has impressed me every time and I cannot speak too highly of him. He is mature beyond his years, he is a great athlete and he has shown he can perform on the big stage.'

After being excluded from the England schoolboy set-up, Gerrard had first played for his country at Under-16 level, then made his mark as captain of the England Under-18s. In March 1999, barely four months after his senior Reds debut, he was invited, along with Leeds defender Jonathan Woodgate, to train with the full England side as they prepared for a European Championship qualifier with Poland. In September of that year, Gerrard made his debut for the Under-21s and scored the opening goal of the game against Luxembourg.

Gerrard's first call-up to the senior squad in February 2000, for England's friendly with Argentina, spelled the beginning of the end of his time with the Under-21s. Only injury prevented him from earning his first senior cap in that game and, following his starring role in the England Under-21s victory over Yugoslavia a month later, he was in line for another call-up as the senior side warmed up for the European Championships with games against Brazil and the Ukraine.

When Howard Wilkinson named his squad for the European Under-21 Championships, Gerrard's name was not read out. Wilkinson admitted that Keegan had specifically asked for Gerrard and fellow Under-21s Emile Heskey, Kieron Dyer and Rio Ferdinand to be left out.

Keegan was eager to give Gerrard his first taste of international football on home soil. The friendlies against Brazil and the Ukraine gave the England head coach the ideal chance to run a final rule over his players before naming his squad.

But, rather like all his other managers, Keegan was reluctant to rush Gerrard in. The Liverpool youngster watched from the bench as England earned a 1–1 draw with Brazil at Wembley – with Michael Owen scoring England's goal. However, Gerrard did not have to wait long to get his first taste of the hallowed Wembley turf.

Keegan handed him his first cap on his 20th birthday, against the Ukraine, while his new England team-mates marked the occasion by filling his trainers with toothpaste. Inspector Gerrard quickly compiled a list of suspects.

'I have asked Robbie Fowler if it was him and he has sworn on his baby's life it wasn't, so it is definitely not him. They broke into my room when I was having a bath. I couldn't put my shoes on because they were so heavy! I don't suspect I will ever find out who it was. It couldn't have been the manager, could it? He gives me my first cap and then does that to me? ... The greatest birthday present I have ever been given was when the manager told me I was in against the Ukraine. I will buy myself a present when I get home. I have already got a Mercedes ordered. There is nothing I want now after being given my first England cap... apart from a new pair of trainers.'

Gerrard and Owen had come a long way with one another since they had sat together as 12-year-olds watching Leeds beat Liverpool in the Charity Shield at Wembley – Gerrard's only previous visit to the home of English football. They were now destined to play there together for England.

Gerrard announced his arrival in the England senior realm with a composed and convincing performance. Robbie Fowler opened the scoring for England, before a second-half Tony Adams strike completed a 2–0 victory.

With that, Keegan included Gerrard in his squad for Euro 2000, but the Liverpool midfielder, following his outstanding international debut, was not prepared to settle for a role as a back-up player. 'Now I'm in the final 22, I just want to play a part in Euro 2000,' he said.

Skipper Tony Adams welcomed Gerrard into the international arena. The Arsenal stalwart revealed, 'I told him, "You know what to do, don't you?" He looked at me and said, "What?" I said, "Panic, but don't bloody pass it to me." It was just something to break the spell. He was OK after that. I told him to go out and enjoy it. It's a special moment for anybody.'

The other 21 players travelling to the European Championships included Owen, Heskey and Fowler, as well as former Anfield stars Paul Ince and Steve McManaman. The 20-year-old Gerrard would be in rousing company.

Drawn against Portugal, Germany and Romania in Group A, England would have to be at their very best if they were to make it through to the quarter-finals. They began in Eindhoven against the Portuguese, a side that was being hotly tipped for glory. Keegan chose Ince to play alongside Manchester United goal-getter Paul Scholes in central midfield and the selection looked to be paying dividends as Scholes and then McManaman put England 2–0 up inside the opening 20 minutes. But a Luis Figo-inspired Portugal hit back to win 3–2 and Keegan was sent back to the drawing board.

Gerrard had not figured in the opening game and his lack of experience counted against him as Keegan considered his options to face Germany in the next game. Many pundits felt Gerrard's energy made him preferable to the ageing Ince in midfield, Alex Ferguson among them.

'I would fancy playing Steven Gerrard as the anchorman midfielder,' the Manchester United manager told the *Sunday Times*. 'He is only 20, but he is physically and technically precocious. He has a good engine and displays remarkable energy on the pitch.'

But the pressure was on Keegan to deliver a team of winners in Charleroi, and he kept faith with Ince. A 1–0 win, courtesy of Alan Shearer, vindicated the manager's decision. But not without Gerrard coming on after an hour to help withstand the battering, as Germany went all out for an equaliser. It was England's first victory over Germany in 34 years.

'Young Gerrard refused to be intimidated by the electric atmosphere in Charleroi and even bossed his much more experienced midfield partners Paul Ince and Dennis Wise around at times,' reported the *News of the World*.

'Steven gave us a cameo of the future of English football,' enthused Keegan.

In hindsight, and to the watching critic, it was much more than that. How sad then, for England, that Keegan could not call upon Gerrard to start the final, crucial group game against Romania due to a niggling thigh strain. A 3–2 defeat, courtesy of a heart-breakingly late penalty, saw England on the early plane home.

For the likes of Gerrard and Owen, two of just a handful of players who came away from the tournament with any credit, the future looked good. However, Kevin Keegan's England career was grinding to a halt.

6

After Euro 2000, Gerrard barely had time to take stock before he was back in training ahead of the new domestic programme. The 2000/01 season was set to be a tremendously telling year, both for him and for Liverpool.

Gérard Houllier had spent £20 million on new players and the signings he had made suggested that Liverpool would finally have a sturdy backbone. The arrival of veteran midfield enforcer Gary McAllister from Coventry was billed as the surprise transfer of the summer, and it was certainly the most significant as far as Gerrard was concerned. Liverpool needed midfield reinforcements and an experienced head to help Gerrard's continuing progress. McAllister, at 35, was a welcome addition to the Liverpool squad.

'Robbie Fowler wears the armband, but as far as I'm concerned Gary is another skipper here,' Gerrard later said. 'Both on the field and in the dressing room he is a massive influence on myself and every other youngster here. It's like walking on to the field on a Saturday and playing beside a coach!'

Gerrard himself signed a lucrative new contract with Liverpool that summer, which allowed him to stop driving his dad's Honda and buy a spanking new car of his own. And he was brimming with excitement over the season that lay ahead.

'I know more will be expected of me this season, but I'm not really one who feels pressure. I like a challenge, and the first one will be trying to play every week for Liverpool because everyone here is such a good player. I know this will be a very big season for me – much bigger than last year – but I'm looking forward to it. I want to play against Vieira and Keane and compare myself with them. One day I will be as good and then be better.'

Gerrard was fit and raring to go; the question was, were Liverpool ready? Houllier had a £50 million squad at his disposal that included a wealth of midfield talent: Nick Barmby, Gary McAllister, Patrick Berger, Dietmar Hamann, Vladimir Smicer, Danny Murphy and Gerrard were all vying for midfield positions in his starting XI.

With expectations high, the Reds began the 2000/01 campaign against Bradford City, the side against whom they had ended the last season. Gerrard partnered Hamann in central midfield, with Barmby and Smicer on the flanks. The eager Anfield spectators were forced to wait for Liverpool to step into their groove, but Gerrard's 48th-minute curling effort – well saved by Bradford goalkeeper Matt Clarke – sparked life into Houllier's men. A stunning display of power and determination saw Emile Heskey score the winner for Liverpool. Gerrard, before making way for McAllister late in the second half, had delivered another dynamic performance and looked increasingly confident – especially when it came to shooting from long range. However, Houllier, incessantly answering questions about his young prodigy, was quick to emphasise the role he, as manager, had to play in Gerrard's continuing development.

'In the 18 to 24 age group, that of Lampard, Carragher, Gerrard, Heskey, Owen, Barry and Joe Cole, the raw material is there to make a good national team. They can be your base. The problem is the way some of them choose to live their lives. I'm talking about what sort of professionals they want to be.

'Steven is a tremendous asset to the club. He's a steady Eddie, so there's no danger of all the publicity spoiling him and, if he stays fit and overcomes the various muscular injuries he gets, he'll be even better than last season.'

Houllier was delighted with his side's winning start to the season, but he was less than impressed with Sky television's orchestration of the fixture list: Liverpool's second match of the season, away to Arsenal, would kick off barely 48 hours after the end of their opening game.

Heskey and Berger had both picked up injuries against Bradford and the Reds were set to start the clash at Highbury without valuable firepower. Houllier employed a 4-5-1 formation against Arsenal and took the bold move of resting Gerrard completely, keeping both him and Michael Owen on the bench. The England pair were badly missed. Arsenal won 2–0 and referee Graham Poll sent off McAllister and Hamann – both for over-elaborate tackling – as well as Arsenal's Patrick Vieira for a nasty two-footed lunge.

Gerrard was named in Kevin Keegan's England squad later that week for a friendly with France. He was joined by the other young starlets who were earmarked to turn England's fortunes around, Kieron Dyer, Rio Ferdinand and Gareth Barry.

On his return to league action, Gerrard was clearly still hampered by his groin, as Liverpool threw away a 3–0 lead at Southampton to finish with just a draw. Houllier urged caution as the star jetted off to join Keegan's squad in Paris. Gerrard was not able to play two games in a week.

Keegan took heed of the situation and agreed that it would be wrong to force Gerrard to play. 'I'll have to have a look at him in training,' he said. 'I've talked to Gérard Houllier and to the Liverpool physio, Dave Galley, and it seems he's still growing and hasn't got all his strength yet. We'll see how he is. I won't do anything to jeopardise his long-term future.'

Gerrard was being hotly tipped to take over from Paul Ince as England's midfield general. 'Incey isn't getting any younger,' Gerrard said. 'But he's still a great player and he's going to fight on for as long as he can. I've got to keep trying to produce the form for Liverpool that has got me this far and hope that that's enough to hold down an England place for years to come.'

Gerrard's dream of facing France – and earning his third England cap – was ultimately thwarted by his unrelenting injury. He was forced to head back to Merseyside for treatment. England earned a 1–1 draw with France and Owen, the goalscorer, was back to his lethal best.

Gerrard returned to the Reds' starting XI and Owen proceeded to fire a shattering first-half hat-trick against

Aston Villa. There was no doubting that the two players, having orchestrated this 3–1 win, were the hub of a side that was about to inflict its potent magic both on English football and on the European stage.

But Gerrard was absent again for Liverpool's long-awaited return to European competition. Nick Barmby was the Reds' goal-scoring hero as they defeated Rapid Bucharest in the UEFA Cup first-round first-leg tie. Little did they know it then, but it heralded the beginning of a magnificent march to glory.

Gerrard had undertaken a week of rest and recuperation before he donned his boots when Liverpool made a Sunday visit to bottom-of-the-table West Ham. It took him just 12 minutes to score the second Liverpool goal of his career, a strike that typified his astuteness. Galloping into the box, he timed his run perfectly to despatch a Danny Murphy cross from eight yards. His joy was tempered in the second half, however, as Paolo Di Canio levelled the score from the penalty spot and he was forced off with a recurrence of an injury problem that was fast becoming a terrible burden.

Gerrard was in and out, showing more and more of his immense potential each time he played, but constantly plagued by the his groin. But there was hope as he came through a bruising encounter with Chelsea unharmed, albeit a 3–0 defeat, and reported fit for England's World Cup qualifier against Germany – the final international at the old Wembley Stadium.

Another recurrence of his groin injury while training at Bisham Abbey ended Gerrard's hopes of playing, and he could only watch as a long-range Dietmar Hamann free-kick evaded the flailing arms of David Seaman and delivered a critical blow to Keegan's reign. The beleaguered manager quit straight after the match, claiming that his role had become untenable. It was a bitterly disappointing end for the manager who had given Gerrard his first opportunity at senior international level.

Howard Wilkinson took up a caretaker role for England's second qualifying game in Finland four days later and an injury-hit side, minus Gerrard, David Beckham and captain Tony Adams, among others, could only see out a goalless draw in Helsinki. The national side were in turmoil and were desperately in need of new spark and invention.

In an effort to ease the strain on Gerrard's groin, Houllier moved him to right-back, where he gave an imperious performance in a 3–1 win over Everton, which left Liverpool third in the table.

'Everyone is buzzing in our dressing room because we've not beaten Everton very often in recent years. And Emile is on fire and proving the critics wrong,' said Gerrard. 'Now it's important we stay in the top three and, although my favourite position is in midfield, I'm quite happy to play at the back when the boss selects me there.'

He was rested the following Wednesday as Chelsea visited Anfield in the third round of the League Cup. Danny Murphy and Robbie Fowler sent Liverpool through after another tempestuous affair, in which Heskey saw red before Fowler struck his first goal of the season in extra-time to put the Reds into the fourth round.

Gerrard returned to the centre of midfield for the UEFA Cup second-round second-leg tie against Slovan Liberec. Peter Taylor, England's interim manager, had named

Gerrard in a strong squad for a friendly with Italy in Turin, and he was out to prove his fitness once and for all. Liverpool fell behind to an early goal but Gerrard inspired a Reds comeback, as goals from Barmby, Heskey and Owen sent Liverpool through. Gerrard was unlucky not to score himself with a couple of long-range efforts as he continued to take a firm grasp of European football.

Three days after their trip to the Czech Republic, Gerrard partnered McAllister in central midfield for the first time, against Coventry City, and the combination worked superbly. Gerrard scored the second goal – his third ever for Liverpool – in a 4–1 rout and received a standing ovation as he was substituted 12 minutes from the end.

Sven-Goran Eriksson had been confirmed as England's future head coach and the Swede was present to see his new charges take on Italy in Turin. Despite Peter Taylor naming a youthful England side for the game, Gerrard's name was not on the team sheet – his international injury jinx had struck again. This time it was a hamstring problem that kept him out of a narrow 1–0 defeat in a game that showed so many encouraging signs for England fans, mainly due to the refreshing injection of youth. The future looked brighter for England, but for Gerrard, who was yet to claim his third cap, his international future remained unclear.

He was back to score his fourth Liverpool goal in a UEFA Cup third-round tie away to Olympiakos – a game dubbed as Liverpool's most arduous European assignment in years. His first-ever European goal was not enough for victory, though, as Olympiakos set up an intriguing second leg with an injury-time equaliser. Liverpool's quest for glory was proving no easy ride.

If Liverpool had let themselves down in the first leg, they more than made up for it when Olympiakos visited Anfield for the crucial second leg. Tord Grip, England's new assistant manager, was in attendance to see Heskey join fellow England star Barmby on the scoresheet as Houllier's side enhanced their trophy-winning credentials with a stunning performance. If Grip had been impressed by Heskey, then he would have been doubly awed by Gerrard's gripping midfield display. Only a remarkable save from a stunning left-foot volley denied him the goal that his performance richly deserved.

Back in the Premiership, Ipswich stunned Liverpool with a 1–0 win at Anfield as the Reds fell awkwardly foul of Houllier's rotation policy. Gerrard, somewhat understandably following his heroics three days earlier, was left as an unused substitute, but Heskey was also named on the bench, much to the surprise of the Liverpool fans. New signing Igor Biscan received his baptism as a second-half replacement, but neither he nor Heskey could turn around an adverse Anfield display.

If that game was tough, then the visit of Fulham provided Liverpool with a further test of resolve in a League Cup quarter-final clash. The Cottagers, who were top of the First Division under Jean Tigana at the time, were more than a match for Liverpool. However, they could not overcome Gerrard's almighty Man of the Match influence. He was in his pomp once again to ensure that Liverpool, already the favourites to win the competition, overcame a particularly high hurdle. Michael Owen, on his

21st birthday, broke the deadlock in extra-time, before Smicer and Barmby put an extra gloss on the scoreline to see Liverpool advance to the semi-final.

Having limped off with cramp minutes from the end of that cup-tie, Gerrard was considered a doubt for Liverpool's trip to face Manchester United. However, he recovered in time and partnered new boy Igor Biscan in midfield as Danny Murphy's memorable free-kick handed the Reds a shock win in Houllier's 100th game in charge.

If Gerrard had been outstanding at Old Trafford against Roy Keane, then he was world class when Arsenal came to Anfield with Patrick Vieira – another of the players he looked up to. What a game, what a performance! If any game signified the true, if tardy, resurgence of Liverpool Football Club under Houllier, then this was it.

Having won at Old Trafford for the first time in ten years, confidence was sky high and title-winning dreams were very much alive. Gerrard personified such hope and, if he hadn't been already, was crowned King of Liverpool's midfield with a stunning goal – his fifth senior strike. Vieira, Arsenal's midfield guru, could only look on in amazement following his poor defensive header, as his young adversary intelligently allowed the ball to drop and, without hesitation, lashed a right-foot bullet past David Seaman into the corner of the net. Such opportunism was to become a mainstay of Gerrard's game.

After Owen had hit Liverpool's second, a typically full-bodied ball-winning tackle from Liverpool's hero of the hour led to Barmby making it 3–0. Gerrard was taken off to a euphoric ovation from the Kop, before Fowler made it 4–0 and sealed the wrapping paper on what had been a blissful Christmas present for the Liverpool fans. 'We are not going to win the league... our target is the top three. But if we keep performing like this, who knows?' said an excited Gerrard after the game.

That optimism was shaken a little by another uncertain display on Boxing Day when Liverpool lost 1–0 to Middlesbrough on Teesside. The Reds were in need of a rest after a strenuous spate of matches, and an unexpected favour from Mother Nature afforded Gerrard and company a chance to recharge their batteries when their scheduled clash with Bradford City at Valley Parade was postponed due to snow.

Fully refuelled, Gerrard broke in 2001 with another sparkling display – arguably his best yet for Liverpool. He proved his class with a one-man show against Southampton at Anfield, culminating in an unstoppable right-footed drive from fully 35 yards into the top-left corner of Paul Jones's goal. 'It could be the goal of the season,' said an admiring Houllier after the game.

But the team as a whole was struggling for consistency. After a relatively routine 3–0 victory over Rotherham in the FA Cup third round, they went to Selhurst Park for the League Cup semi-final first leg and lost 2–1 to First Division Crystal Palace.

A critical match at Aston Villa in the Premiership then saw new signing Jari Litmanen make his debut, but his class was eclipsed by another sterling display from Gerrard, whose long-range shooting was fast becoming his hallmark. Sandwiched in between a terrific double by Murphy came another Gerrard rocket from the edge of the box, his sixth goal of the season.

STEVEN GERRARD

Liverpool, by now, were second only to Manchester United in the Premiership goal-scoring charts. And they showed their credentials in the second leg of their League Cup semi-final tie with Crystal Palace, turning round the 2–1 first-leg deficit with a 5–0 victory that secured their place in the Worthington Cup final.

Gerrard's hopes of making Eriksson's squad for a friendly against Spain were cast into doubt when he limped out of Liverpool's 1–1 draw with Sunderland at the Stadium of Light. And worse heartache was to follow when he was forced to remain at home for treatment while Liverpool flew to Italy for a UEFA Cup fourth-round first-leg clash with Roma. The groin injury that had dogged him almost relentlessly had returned with a vengeance.

The Reds were able to combat his absence somewhat with the return to action of Michael Owen, who scored two goals as Liverpool beat Roma 2–0 in the Olympic Stadium. Liverpool then progressed to the quarter-finals of the FA Cup with a 4–2 defeat of Manchester City at Anfield, again without Gerrard, but the Kop's dream of silverware was very much alive, with a possible treble of League Cup, FA Cup and UEFA Cup growing ever more real.

That tantalising prospect nearly fell flat when Roma visited Anfield for the UEFA Cup fourth-round second leg – a game where Gerrard's prolonged absence finally told. The Italians sneaked a 1–0 win on the night and went mightily close to forcing a below-par Liverpool into extra-time. But the Reds had earned a place in the quarter-finals of the UEFA Cup. In front of them, though, was the Worthington Cup final.

Gerrard had been cast as a serious doubt for the showpiece but, after some near-non-stop treatment at Melwood, he was passed fit for his first-ever cup final. He was put on the right side of midfield as Houllier sought to get the best out of his team's creativity against their opponents, First Division Birmingham City.

Robbie Fowler put the Reds ahead with a stunning volley, before a penalty deep in second-half stoppage time from Darren Purse sent the game into extra-time. Well before that, Gerrard had hobbled off, suffering another relapse of his groin problem; it was a moment that signalled a decline in Liverpool's hold on the match. Too many games too young was the simple diagnosis.

At least Liverpool had the ever-ready McAllister in reserve to take the youngster's place. Despite his pain, Gerrard mounted the podium at the end of the match to pick up his first winners' medal, after Liverpool won in a dramatic penalty shoot-out. Trophy number one.

Gerrard was back in Liverpool's midfield when they met Leicester at Filbert Street in March. Entering their most important period in years, Liverpool lost 2–0 to the struggling Foxes with Gerrard failing to provide his side with any spark alongside McAllister. Liverpool slipped from third to fourth and, with their title aspirations all but extinguished, question marks now hung over their Champions League qualification as well.

Porto were Liverpool's quarter-final opponents in the UEFA Cup, and the Reds came back from the first leg in Portugal with a creditable goalless draw. They were now firm favourites to progress.

A clue to Gerrard's ongoing injury problems came with

the revelation that he had undergone a growth spurt that had added three inches to his height and a stone to his weight in just 12 months.

'When I was 15, I was the same size as Michael Owen, but he is a midget next to me now,' he beamed to the gathered media at a press conference. 'The rapid growth has given me posture problems and my muscles get tired, but it is getting better. It is impossible to put a date on when it will be perfect, but I am playing more games this season than I did last time.'

Gerrard wasn't just growing physically; his reputation was also growing at a phenomenal rate. After playing against him, Porto defender Fernando Nelson said, 'Gerrard makes Liverpool tick.'

He was making them tick again as they beat Merseyside neighbours Tranmere 4–2 in the FA Cup quarter-final, with Gerrard scoring his first FA Cup goal, and his seventh of the season. Just three days later, Liverpool made it into the semi-finals of the UEFA Cup by seeing off Porto at Anfield. Owen and Murphy scored on a night of spine-tingling excitement, but again it was Gerrard who rose to take the responsibility of firing Liverpool forward on his own young shoulders. Playing his fifth full game in a row, he teed up both goals with crosses of devastating accuracy. Sven-Goran Eriksson was in the crowd.

Crucially, for Gerrard at least, he was fit and ready for England's World Cup qualifying matches against Finland and Albania – and also Liverpool's looming UEFA Cup semi-final tie against Spanish giants Barcelona. He was excited about playing a full game for England for the first time, and had been visiting an orthopaedic specialist in

France to try to combat his injury worries. The treatment had done him good.

'I am fine,' he said. 'There is no injury problem. I am fit and available and ready to play for England if I am selected... I desperately want to play.'

Gerrard's 17 starts in his last 20 games suggested that he was a little more agile than most, including Houllier, appeared to think. However, on the other side of England's brace of World Cup qualifying matches lay Liverpool's biggest league game of the season – a home game with rivals Manchester United. Houllier's fears were perhaps understandable.

Gerrard passed a late fitness test to line up for England at Anfield – a fitting venue for him to shrug off all doubt and earn his third England cap, while Eriksson took charge of his new-look side for the first time in a competitive game.

'All the best... have a nightmare on Saturday,' had been Gerrard's cheeky final words to Finnish Liverpool team-mate Sami Hyypia before the match. However mischievous that was, Gerrard was more of a nuisance on the field. His lion-like display was only upstaged by an awesome performance by David Beckham. England fell behind to an early own goal by Gary Neville, but Michael Owen equalised before Beckham, the new England skipper, won the game with a trademark curling effort. Gerrard did well to marshal England's midfield with authority alongside Paul Scholes. And with Scholes licensed to go forward, Gerrard was left with the responsibility of frustrating his Anfield colleague Jari Litmanen, Finland's key player, and, in doing so, he completed 90 minutes in an England shirt for the very first time.

But he needed a rest, and so Eriksson called upon Nicky Butt to take Gerrard's place in Albania, where England came away with an unconvincing 3–1 victory.

A week's rest gave Gerrard the chance to recuperate for Liverpool's much-publicised clash with Manchester United. Keen to stir things up ahead of the potentially explosive clash, the newspapers drew blood from both sides of the M6. Gerrard was particularly looking forward to his meeting with Roy Keane.

Gerrard's perceptible improvements in all aspects of his game were earning praise of the highest order from across the football spectrum. Sir Bobby Robson echoed the sentiment that Gerrard was reminiscent of Bryan Robson. 'He possesses the four Cs in abundance: courage, consistency, confidence and class,' said the former England manager, who had relied on Robson just as Houllier relied on Gerrard.

All four of those attributes oozed from Gerrard as Manchester United fell before his warrior-like leadership at Anfield. He set Liverpool on their way to an illustrious victory when he scored arguably the finest goal of the 2000/01 Premiership season. Fully 32 yards from goal, he unleashed a 67mph thunderbolt that rocketed past United's Fabien Barthez in the blink of an eye.

'I think it was my best goal for Liverpool so far,' stated Gerrard later.

More was to come. The roving midfielder supplied a deft pass for Fowler to notch and send Anfield wild. With that, Liverpool had completed a sensational double over their arch-rivals – a feat not achieved by them for 22 years. Anfield, quite rightly, lauded the contribution of the 20-

year-old who had proved, if he hadn't already, that he was a colossus in mind, body and soul.

If that was a big game, then Barcelona away in a UEFA Cup semi-final was monstrous. The Reds flew to Spain with one primary objective: to defend and earn a mouth-watering second-leg tie at Anfield. For Gerrard, it was a chance to shine in one of the finest stadiums in the world – and how he graced the Nou Camp with his iridescent, youthful brilliance.

Many pundits, in the build-up to the UEFA Cup semi-final, saw this game as Gerrard's acid test – an opportunity to find out just how good he really was. Before the game, Barcelona had singled him out as a potential primary tormentor.

'I thought Liverpool looked very good against Manchester United at the weekend and I was particularly impressed by Steven Gerrard,' defender Michael Reiziger warned. 'He looks like he has everything he needs to make a great midfielder and at such a young age. Judging by the quality of that goal he scored, I think he's the one we need to stop.'

Barcelona did, at least, prevent him from scoring on a balmy night in Spain, but a goalless draw nudged Liverpool a little closer to European glory.

Houllier had to take his players off the European pedestal swiftly as Liverpool's marathon season continued at Villa Park in an FA Cup semi-final against Second Division troopers Wycombe Wanderers. Gerrard, somewhat understandably, was rested, although he did appear as a second-half substitute to set up a goal for Emile Heskey, as the Reds made the final with a 2–1 victory.

With one trophy in the bag, another final lined up and a third within touching distance, Liverpool's season was coming to an epic climax. But mounting fixture congestion gave Houllier reason to be unsettled. How could he rest his most influential stars, in particular Gerrard, as Liverpool entered their most important spell in near on a decade? The answer was simple – he couldn't. Even the league required their best efforts if they were to secure the Champions League spot they so craved.

Barely 48 hours after the FA Cup semi-final, the Reds were at Portman Road for a crucial Premiership encounter with Ipswich. And their tired legs could only muster a 1–1 draw; Gerrard teed up Heskey for Liverpool's solitary goal. The Reds' Champions League qualification hopes took a further blow three days later when Leeds came to Anfield and won 2–1. Gerrard scored Liverpool's goal but ended a miserable afternoon with his second dismissal for Liverpool, following a second booking. Next up, a Merseyside derby at Goodison Park.

Having played three games in five days, Gerrard was excused more bodily punishment in the Merseyside derby. Liverpool had slipped to sixth in the Premiership table and simply had to beat Everton to revive their Champions League qualification hopes. Gerrard's exclusion seemingly made that task a whole lot harder.

Igor Biscan stepped into midfield alongside McAllister, and, if the acquisition of McAllister needed any justification, then Liverpool had to look no further than the 36-year-old's 94th-minute free-kick that earned the Reds a stunning 3–2 victory and put their league form back on track.

'This is a new generation of Liverpool players. It is now down to them to make a name for themselves,' said Houllier, upon handing Gerrard a recall for the monumental matter of Liverpool's 23rd cup tie of the season – the second leg of the UEFA Cup semi-final against Barcelona.

Gerrard passed a late fitness test and played an integral role on the right side of midfield as Liverpool made their first European final in 16 years. His industry led to the Reds' decisive goal after he cleverly won a corner on the right-hand side. McAllister's delivery was handled by Barcelona's Patrick Kluivert and the Scottish veteran slammed the resulting penalty into the net for his second crucial goal in the space of four days. Liverpool were through to the UEFA Cup final and an extraordinary Treble lay in reach.

Yet the primary objective, for Houllier at least, remained to qualify for the Champions League. McAllister continued his imperious form, inspiring Liverpool to a run of five successive league wins that saw them leap back into third place.

When Chelsea ended the run with a 2–2 draw at Anfield, it was Liverpool's 60th game of the season. Tired but still battling, they had it all to play for. Their Champions League hopes now rested on their final-day trip to Charlton Athletic. But before that they had the small matter of two major cup finals to attend to.

The Reds prepared to face Arsenal at the Millennium Stadium with the belief that a decade of anonymity was nearing its timely end. The emergence of Gerrard had played a substantial role in propelling Liverpool forward that season, and, coupled with the goal-scoring magic of

Michael Owen, Liverpool's true overwhelming power was instantly recognisable – as Arsenal discovered in Cardiff.

Around 35,000 Liverpool fans descended on Cardiff for the Reds' first FA Cup final since 1996 and they were treated to a classic. Gerrard rarely broke forward in the game, pegged back by Arsenal's armoury of attacking talent. Critics suggested that Patrick Vieira had had the better of the midfield duel over 90 minutes, and after the game Gerrard was gracious enough to admit, 'I learned what a great player Patrick Vieira is – a lot better than me. I went out determined to run the game, win the midfield battle and show everyone the progress I have made this season. But Vieira wouldn't let me do it... Yes, he gave me a bit of a lesson in the cup final but, at the end of it all, I was still the one with the medal.'

Indeed he was. Because, despite the best efforts of Vieira, they couldn't prevent Michael Owen from volleying home an equaliser after a Gary McAllister free-kick had caused mayhem in the box. Then, with just two minutes remaining, Owen latched on to Patrick Berger's long clearance and found the far corner of David Seaman's goal from an almost impossible angle. Gerrard was one of the first to congratulate his best friend on the brace that won the pair their first-ever FA Cup winners' medal.

'Tell me ma, me ma, to put the champagne on ice, we're going to Cardiff twice,' beamed the Liverpool fans, celebrating their two trips to Wales that season. It was a spellbinding climax to a domestic season that had seen Liverpool roll back the years to days of old, where trophy-winning was the norm. The Reds had become only the second English team to win the League Cup and FA Cup in the same season. With two items of gleaming silverware added to the famous Anfield trophy room, Gerrard and his team-mates now turned their attention to the UEFA Cup final.

The final hurdle in a remarkable Treble threw up unpredictable opposition in the form of little-known Spanish giant-killers Alaves. And Gerrard, having struggled to weave his magic against the might of Patrick Vieria in Cardiff, now faced a very different proposition in Alaves' influential Yugoslav midfielder Ivan Tomic – on loan to the Basque side from Roma.

Gerrard, who had been crowned PFA Young Player of the Year, was adamant his side could win their 25th cup tie of the season and complete the Treble.

'If we show the same character as we showed on Saturday in Cardiff, then we will win the UEFA Cup as well,' he said. 'The FA Cup final was special, the highlight of my career, but I hope things will get even better on Wednesday, and then on Saturday against Charlton.'

Out of all the many games Liverpool had played that season, the penultimate proved the most enthralling contest of them all. The Reds were on their game, but so were Alaves. Gary McAllister was drafted into the side, giving the Reds extra midfield bite. That meant Gerrard was moved out to the right of midfield, where he had flourished so often.

Houllier's team selection appeared justified when Liverpool raced into a two-goal lead inside 16 minutes in the Westfalenstadion. McAllister set up Markus Babbel to head in the first after just four minutes, and then Gerrard, with a formidable surging run, took a clever pass from

Michael Owen and buried the ball past Alaves' stricken custodian Martin Herrera. His tenth Liverpool goal of the season, and his second in European competition, gave the Reds what appeared to be a comfortable cushion.

However, Alaves had other ideas, and Ivan Alonso, moments after coming on as a substitute, headed past Sander Westerveld with 27 minutes on the clock. McAllister's penalty, after Owen had been fouled, reaffirmed Liverpool's advantage prior to half-time, but Javi Moreno, Alaves' main marksman, hit a quick-fire double early in the second half to draw the Spaniards level.

Liverpool's enterprising qualities were tested to the limit again, but an old hero was on hand to put them ahead again. Robbie Fowler, who had been left out of the starting line-ups for both the UEFA and FA Cup finals, leaped off the bench to score with a splendid left-foot drive from the edge of the area in the 73rd minute to the delight of the Reds' 20,000 travelling fans.

Fowler's goal epitomised Liverpool's fighting spirit, but whatever Gérard Houllier's side did that night, Alaves matched, and Jordi Cruyff's late header sent an already remarkable contest into extra-time, with the score level at 4–4.

Liverpool gained the upper hand in additional time when Alaves' Cosmin Contra was sent off. And the pulsating match would not have been complete without a last-gasp winner. Fate and fortune ensured that it would be Liverpool who took home the honours: McAllister's curling free-kick from wide left was inadvertently flicked on by Delfi Geli and the ball ended up in the back of the net. An own goal it was, and this time there was no way back for the courageous Spaniards – Liverpool were Treble winners, having won their first European trophy in 17 years.

The Liverpool players returned home to a rapturous reception, but, for the time being, celebrating the completion of such a remarkable achievement remained on hold: there was still one more critical match left – arguably the biggest of them all.

If Liverpool didn't qualify for the Champions League, then their season, at least in terms of solid progression, would have been deemed a failure. A massive game awaited them at The Valley on the final day of the season – Charlton Athletic away. Liverpool's 63rd and last game of the campaign would be no simple task.

Extra-time in Dortmund had done enough to send legs dizzy and emotions drained. The likes of McAllister and Gerrard, who had toiled tirelessly, not just in that game but for the entire season, had to deliver one final time. The tiredness showed in south-east London but, in truth, the Reds were probably only conserving their energy for the second-half storm that swept them into the Champions League.

Houllier, claiming his players were 'playing for immortality', reinstated Fowler into his line-up and it was he who galvanised the Reds. A superbly crafted volley and a low drive put Liverpool in the driving seat. Sandwiched in between Fowler's brace was a 20-yard screamer from Danny Murphy, before Owen rounded off an incredible year by making it 4–0, as cries of 'Three cups and the Champions League' emanated from the jubilant Liverpool fans who had seen their side beat Leeds into third place.

Steven Gerrard in 1990, aged 10. Like many football-mad youngsters he proudly wore a replica England shirt. His youthful talent, however, had already marked him out as a special lad.

Above: Instrumental in championing Gerrard's cause was Steve Heighway, former player and School of Excellence coach at Liverpool FC.

Right: Already displaying his future trademark qualities, a domineering midfield performance marked Gerrard's second game in the England U21 side, against Poland in September 1999.

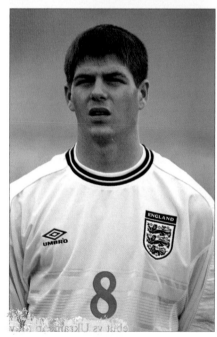

Above: Steven Gerrard and Denmark's Claus Jensen battle for the ball during an England U21 friendly in October 1999.

Below: The day after his 20th birthday, Gerrard lines up before his senior England debut at line in May 2000.

Above: England vs Ukraine. Gerrard showed confidence and the ability to run with the ball on his senior debut.

Below: Gerrard and defensive stalwart Tony Adams sit out training during Euro 2000 in Belgium. Adams proved a steadying influence on the young Gerrard in the early days of the Merseysider's international career.

At the end of the 2000/01 season, Gerrard deservedly received the prestigious Professional Football Association Young Player of the Year Award.

Gerrard has always been careful to preserve his mobility. Here he stretches during England team training at the end of August 2004.

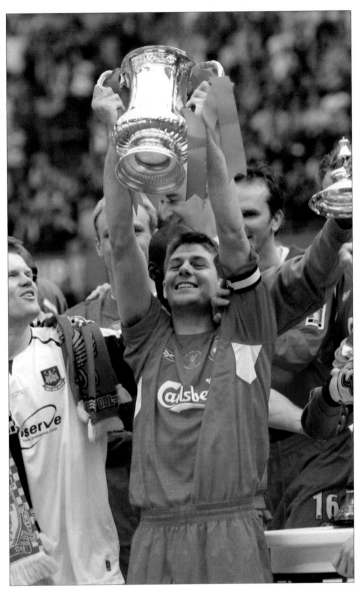

Steven proudly holds aloft the FA Cup after Liverpool's dramatic
victory over West Ham in the 2006 final.

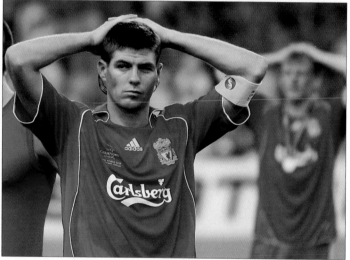

Bitter disappointment followed for Gerrard as he missed a penalty during England's world cup exit against Portugal in 2006 (*above*) and as he failed to recapture the magic of Istanbul in the 2007 Champions League final (*below*). Like any truly great player, the setbacks will only strengthen Gerrard's determination to make Liverpool the best team in the land in the seasons to come.

Gerrard and his fellow heroes returned to Merseyside for the biggest celebration Liverpool had seen in years. The open-top bus that paraded them around the streets of the city barely had room for the three trophies and all the people that had contributed to an unimaginable achievement. At the front of the bus, manager Gérard Houllier held aloft the UEFA Cup, Robbie Fowler waved the FA Cup and a beaming and proud Gerrard flaunted the League Cup.

'This season has not been a victory for 11 or 14 players, it is for the entire group,' exclaimed Houllier. 'When you have the skill, and on top of that the will, you'll achieve. We have come through because of the belief the players have in themselves and the trust they have in each other.'

Liverpool had astounded even their own hardy supporters. So too had a 20-year-old who had overcome injury to put himself in the highest echelons of Europe's best midfield players. In total, Gerrard started 29 league games in the 2000/01 season, making four appearances as a substitute, scoring seven Premiership goals and spending a total of 2,529 minutes on the pitch. He picked up just four bookings in those games, and saw red on one occasion. In cup competition, he hit three goals as part of his contribution to Liverpool's Treble triumph. A total of 11 goals and near on 50 club appearances was an amazing input from a player labelled a liability because of his injury problems.

With the champagne corks still popping, Liverpool's contingent of England stars headed off on international duty for a friendly against Mexico. A crucial World Cup qualifier with Greece was to follow closely behind. Having proven his potency at club level, Gerrard now relished his chance to rubber-stamp his position at the heart of England's midfield.

Mexico were torn apart by England at Derby's Pride Park. And Gerrard, five days ahead of his 21st birthday, was at the pinnacle of their activity: having combined with midfield cohort Paul Scholes to set up a goal for the Manchester United star, and then crossing for Robbie Fowler to score England's second, he came agonisingly close to firing home his first England goal before wholesale half-time changes saw him replaced by Liverpool team-mate Jamie Carragher. David Beckham and Teddy Sheringham scored a dazzling free-kick apiece to round off a fabulous 4–0 victory.

The man who had been responsible for helping Gerrard overcome his injury problems was Dr Philippe Boixel. The Liverpool hero visited the French guru every three weeks in the French town of Laval for some painstaking manipulation of his troublesome back. The medical expert, personal trainer to some of the best players on the planet, revealed that his client was winning his fight against the problem.

'Steven Gerrard is a great talent, but he can only express himself fully when he is free of pain. The problem has arisen from injuries he suffered early in his career. It could have been something as simple as a twisted ankle to start with. What has happened is that, as a reaction to injuries of that kind, he has developed what we call a bad posture. The position of his body is not as it should be. It goes back some years. That, in itself, brings fatigue on more quickly and, when the muscles are tired, they are more prone to damage. It's only by constant manipulation and monitoring of the spine that Steven can improve.'

Judging by the extensive mileage Gerrard had clocked up that season compared to the previous one, it seemed the treatment he had been receiving was proving its worth. Thanks to Boixel, England's World Cup qualifier with Greece in Athens saw the England midfielder complete back-to-back international appearances for the first time in his career.

Gerrard was resigned to celebrating his 21st birthday at England's training camp in the Spanish resort of La Manga. Despite being pictured toasting the occasion opening a magnum of champagne, he was not allowed to consume any of the contents. Eriksson didn't want to compromise his flourishing partnership with Paul Scholes in the heart of England's midfield.

'Gerrard and Scholes are technically both good on the ball. They are both good passers, hard workers and can shoot well. They can do everything; they are very modern midfielders. I've never had this kind of situation in the past where my teams have boasted two excellent midfielders who are equally good at getting forward and tracking back.'

David Beckham, the new England captain, was equally enthusiastic. 'Stevie is the best young player in England. He's a great talent. He has proved that in the games he has played for us. No one is stopping him. He's such a powerful runner for a young lad.'

Alongside Beckham and Scholes, Gerrard combined to nullify Greece's midfield in Athens as England made further progress towards qualifying for the 2002 World

Cup. A 2–0 victory, thanks to a goal from Scholes and a typically divine Beckham free-kick, put the Eriksson era in full motion. Gerrard's raking passes, tough tackling and all-round maturity exemplified a thoroughly professional performance. Confidence under the new manager was high.

'This is a very exciting time for the whole country,' said Gerrard. 'The rest of the world has been watching our games. They know we have improved a lot and are going to get even better. And I think that will scare a few teams off. I don't think we are far away from winning things with this team. Maybe this World Cup might be a bit too soon, but, if we keep improving and developing, I don't see why we can't go and win it in 2006.'

England's next World Cup qualifier would be against Germany in Munich – on paper, the most challenging of all their group games. With Greece brushed aside, Gerrard and company could, at last, sit back and reflect on a gruelling, yet rewarding, season.

7

Barely four weeks after England's game with Greece, Liverpool were back in pre-season training. Jamie Redknapp had returned from injury after missing out on the whole of the Treble-winning campaign, and he was joined by some new faces on Melwood's manicured training pitches. Norwegian wide man John Arne Riise had been signed from Monaco, followed by Chris Kirkland, the young Coventry goalkeeper, and also the Polish goalie Jerzy Dudek. Christian Zeige was the only major name to leave, as Gérard Houllier sought the same kindred spirit in his squad that had reaped so many rewards the year before.

Redknapp's return to action proved a timely blessing; only one week into the preparations, Gerrard, who had put pen to paper on a new contract committing himself to Anfield until 2005, was nursing another injury, this time to his ankle. He picked it up while he was at Liverpool's training camp in Switzerland and the early prognosis suggested that the England star would be out of action for a prolonged period.

'It is a big blow,' said a despondent Houllier. 'We have a heavy programme in August, but it looks as though he will be absent for a minimum of six weeks.'

Without Gerrard, Liverpool gained more silverware by winning the Charity Shield with a 2–1 victory over Manchester United in Cardiff, then saw off West Ham in similar fashion as they began their assault on the Premiership at Anfield.

Gerrard eventually returned to action as a 72nd-minute substitute for Redknapp in the second leg of Liverpool's Champions League qualifier against FC Haka at Anfield. Houllier's side were already leading 5–0 from the first leg in Finland, so a 4–1 victory at Anfield more than confirmed Liverpool's place in the group stages of Europe's most prestigious competition.

If there had been any doubt about Liverpool's potential in the Champions League, then it was firmly laid to rest in the European Super Cup final in Monaco. Bayern Munich, the reigning champions of Europe, were the opponents, but it was the UEFA Cup holders who reigned in the Stade Louis II with a 3–2 victory. Gerrard made his first start of the season and it took him only 22 minutes to break down a Bayern attack and conjure a fabulously weighted pass to enable Michael Owen to tee up John Arne Riise for the Reds' opening goal.

Such telepathy between the two England men boded well for the forthcoming showdown with Germany. Having proved his fitness, Gerrard was raring for an England return. He had sat frustrated the last time the two teams had met when his Liverpool team-mate Dietmar Hamann's solitary strike brought down the curtain on Kevin Keegan's spell as England manager.

'I sat in the stands and watched at Wembley and it was devastating – a bad day for the country. It would be nice to get one over on Germany because Didi rubbed it in a little bit when they won at Wembley.'

On 1 September 2001, Munich's Olympic Stadium buzzed in anticipation as England took to the field with Germany. Never in their wildest dreams could an England follower have envisaged what was about to happen. Any forecast that this game was going to be anything less than difficult was seemingly blown out of the window when Carsten Jancker prodded Germany ahead inside five minutes.

Far from being overawed by the early sucker punch, England roared back in style. Sven-Goran Eriksson, in his nine or so months in charge, had instilled a sense of unity in his side and it was the Liverpool contingent that united to electrify a stunning fightback.

Michael Owen levelled with a typical poacher's goal. With their tails up, Eriksson's side nudged towards half-time baying for the lead. Two minutes and 31 seconds into stoppage time at the end of the first half, Jens Nowotny, the German centre-back, scythed down David Beckham on England's right side. The captain's initial free-kick delivery was headed away by Dietmar Hamann but, upon retrieving the ball, he got a second chance to cross on his left foot. Rio Ferdinand leaped up on the edge of the penalty area to guide Beckham's centre into the path of Gerrard, who was lurking like a predator 30 yards from goal and seemed to have read exactly what the Leeds United defender was going to do. From that moment on, it was all Gerrard. He deftly controlled the ball on his chest and, with the most adept technical ability, arrowed a low shot via a crowd of players into the bottom right corner of Oliver Kahn's goal.

Gerrard's first-ever England goal, a moment of sheer genius, had England 2–1 ahead at half-time in Munich.

'Rio Ferdinand deserves a lot of credit for the goal,' said Gerrard later. 'As the ball came over I asked him to set it. He set it up perfectly for me to chest down and hit it into the bottom corner. It was a great time to score, to give the lads a boost at half-time. We came out and played a lot better in the second half.'

Owen made it 3–1 shortly after half-time, and, on 66 minutes, comparisons to that epic World Cup final in 1966 were well and truly invoked when Owen matched Geoff Hurst's achievement by completing his hat-trick. And who better than his best friend and long-time club companion to supply the pass that afforded him the chance. In 1966, it had been West Ham's heroes who had shone for England; now it was Liverpool's, with Emile Heskey joining in the fun with England's fifth goal. Germany had been quite remarkably humbled.

'I said we could be better man for man than Germany and we proved that was right tonight,' said a jubilant Gerrard. 'They were on their own soil and we knew they were confident, but we were a lot stronger than the last time we played them at Wembley. There is nothing we can't achieve if we play like this now.'

Gerrard had been spared the final 13 minutes in Munich, in order to save his tired legs from harm for the game against Albania, which was next on England's World Cup qualifying agenda. Gerrard put in a Man of the Match performance as Owen and Fowler scored the goals to give England a 2–0 win at St James' Park. By playing back-to-back matches for England in the space of five days, Gerrard had reached a personal milestone in his battle with injury.

His return to action with Liverpool was less inspiring. Frustrated by his team's stuttering performance at home to Aston Villa, he committed a late, knee-high lunge on George Boateng after 74 minutes and was sent off. Liverpool lost 3–1, their second successive defeat in the league.

A 1–1 draw with Portuguese champions Boavista followed, as Liverpool began their Champions League challenge. Gerrard was restored to a central midfield berth and his engineering crafted a stunning equalising goal for Michael Owen, but it did little to lift the gloom of the previous weekend. What Liverpool needed was a Merseyside derby to reinvigorate their senses and to kick-start their season.

Everton welcomed Liverpool to Goodison Park with a goal from Kevin Campbell after just five minutes, but blue joy in the 165th meeting between the two sides was short-lived – Gerrard had a score to settle. After just 12 minutes, he pounced on a clearance by David Unsworth, shuffled away from Gary Naysmith and crashed a rising drive into the Everton net to set Liverpool on their way to a 3–1 victory. It was his first goal in a Merseyside derby, a sweet moment for any lifelong Liverpool fan.

Greece, an unpredictable European side at the best of times, came to Old Trafford intent on blotting Sven-Goran Eriksson's copybook. The Greeks twice took the lead, either side of an equaliser from Teddy Sheringham, against a lacklustre England. How the home side needed its heroes to deliver.

Before the game, Gerrard had made the headlines after an alleged late-night drinking binge while out with his then girlfriend Jennifer Ellison in Southport. He admitted after the game at Old Trafford that the criticism he received that week had made him realise exactly what he had to lose.

'Everything that has happened to me might act as a jolt. To be honest, I didn't really think I had done anything wrong. I went out for a meal with my girlfriend and friends, and I wasn't drunk or anything like that. I would say the timing wasn't the best, but I don't think I was guilty of anything more than being a bit naive. These are the things that happen when you are a young player and you have to learn from them.

'I intend to do that, because the last few days haven't been nice. Until this week, I didn't realise how people will deliberately go out of their way to make trouble for you.

'People have talked about me in the same category as David Beckham and Michael Owen, which is nice – and I wouldn't have it any other way, because they are the best players in the country, so I have to start behaving like them.'

Against Greece, Beckham had given a masterclass in leadership, saving England's bacon with his tireless running and a fabulous free-kick at the death, which levelled the scores and booked England's place at the World Cup.

The only player misbehaving at Anfield as Liverpool began their defence of the Worthington Cup was Grimsby's Phil Jevons. A lifelong Liverpool fan, dumped by the club as a youngster, he hit a superb 35-yard goal to send the Reds out of the competition. The misery of that night was compounded in very different circumstances when Liverpool hosted Leeds. Houllier was taken to hospital after suffering chest pains at half-time. Phil Thompson, his assistant, oversaw Gerrard's return to Premiership action in Liverpool's 1–1 draw but, for once at least, football was not at the forefront of Anfield minds.

Houllier needed surgery for a hole in his heart, leaving Thompson to guide Liverpool onwards. He took the Reds to the Ukraine to face Dynamo Kiev and sent home the perfect 'Get well soon' card in the shape of a 2–1 win, the winning goal – his first in the competition – scored by a rampant Gerrard.

'Everyone was down in the mouth before the game,' admitted Gerrard. 'It's been a bad few days for us, but we'll dedicate that performance to the gaffer. Hopefully now he'll be on the up and will recover 100 per cent.'

Gerrard's desire to give Houllier yet more cheer was hampered by a sore hamstring that ended his involvement at half-time in Liverpool's 4–1 victory at Leicester – a game which saw Robbie Fowler bag a hat-trick and Jamie Redknapp make his first Premiership start in a year and a half. Gerrard was also left at home for treatment as Liverpool drew 1–1 with Boavista in Portugal the following Wednesday. He returned to set up a goal for Redknapp as Liverpool continued their good form with a 2–0 victory at Charlton in front of a watching Sven-Goran Eriksson.

Four days later, Liverpool honoured Gérard Houllier in the best possible way when they qualified for the second stage of the Champions League by beating Borussia Dortmund 2–0. Gerrard was forced off after a lunge by Dortmund's Dede but, with his brawny frame now able to recover from any slight knock like never before, he was fully fit to face Manchester United at Anfield with Liverpool's title-winning credentials set to be examined under the microscope. A 3–1 victory over United, enough to stir the senses of even the most pessimistic of Liverpool followers, epitomised the sheer potential of the Reds' players, both individually and collectively.

Back-to-back 1–0 victories over Sunderland and Derby, plus a 2–0 victory against Middlesbrough, put Liverpool on top of the Premiership, but then an indifferent run of form prior to Christmas, a spell that included a 4–0 defeat at Chelsea, severely dented the Reds' title aspirations.

Their league form improved in the New Year, including a double over Manchester United, but they were dumped out of the FA Cup by Arsenal, in a match that saw three players sent off, including Jamie Carragher for throwing a coin into the Highbury crowd. Gerrard, still hampered by niggling injuries, was in and out. He eventually returned to training at Melwood ahead of Liverpool's crucial Champions League second-phase match against Barcelona at the Nou Camp. He played a key role in a 0–0 draw against the Catalan giants, although he did reassure all Reds fans that he was human, with a couple of glaring misses that cost Liverpool all three points. Liverpool would have to beat Roma at Anfield in their final second-phase match to progress to the quarter-finals.

Their task was made all the more unenviable by the absence of Michael Owen but, nevertheless, inspired by a return to Anfield for Gérard Houllier, who watched from the stands, Liverpool prevailed 2–0.

The joy of that remarkable night was short-lived for Gerrard. He was forced to limp out of Liverpool's crucial home Premiership match with Chelsea after just 28 minutes, and had to withdraw from the England squad preparing for a friendly with Italy at Elland Road. He cut a forlorn figure as he left the field in a game that Liverpool won 1–0 to move back to the top of the Premiership. Having only just recovered from three weeks on the sidelines, another injury set-back already placed question marks over his involvement in the World Cup, which was now only a couple of months away.

The Champions League remained an appetising prospect, and Gerrard returned for Liverpool's quarter-final first leg at home to Bayer Leverkusen. By virtue of a goal from defender Sami Hyypia and a typically dynamic performance from Gerrard, Liverpool beat the Germans 1–0. But a 4–2 defeat in the return leg a week later curtailed their Champions League dream.

With Houllier now recovered and back at the helm, Liverpool focused on the race for the title. Michael Owen, in a rich vein of form, scored twice as Liverpool defeated Derby 2–0 at Anfield to complete their seventh consecutive win in the Premiership. With the finishing line in sight, they were serious contenders, along with Manchester United and Arsenal. However, a 1–0 defeat by Spurs at White Hart Lane left Liverpool's dream all but shattered, with Gerrard again forced to miss a crucial game due to a groin strain.

But there was joy for Gerrard soon afterwards when Eriksson named him in his 23-man squad for the World

Cup. And when the Reds thrashed Ipswich 5–0 on the final day of the season to clinch second place behind Arsenal, it capped a season that, while it lacked the silverware bonanza of the previous campaign, had marked another big step in the resurgence of Liverpool Football Club under Gérard Houllier.

But Gerrard's sizeable contribution to that feat was about to end in ultimate heartbreak. He had lasted for only 33 minutes against Ipswich, before limping off down the tunnel in obvious discomfort. It was becoming clear that the only thing that would sort out his groin problem once and for all was surgery.

Eriksson, understandably concerned about the threat to one of his star players, said, 'It would be a gamble to take him. Liverpool have been worried since February... I spoke to Steven and he's very down. The best thing now is that he sees the surgeon... I don't know how much it damages our chances.'

Eriksson and England waited with bated breath while Gerrard travelled to Belgium to meet muscular specialist Dr Mark Martens to learn his fate. One scan was all the doctor needed to tell the Liverpool hero, on the eve of his 22nd birthday, that his World Cup dream was over. Immediate surgery was required.

Putting on a brave face, Gerrard said, 'In the short term it is a big blow, but I realise I would have been unable to do myself or the team justice in Japan. The rehabilitation period for this type of operation is six weeks, so my target now is to be fit for the start of next season. I'm confident surgery will cure the problem, so I shall be available for other big tournaments in the future.'

With that, a player who had never experienced defeat in an England shirt was forced to stay at home, toast the beginning of the 23rd year of his life, and watch England on television as they reached out for glory in Japan. Ironically, it was Gerrard's replacement in midfield, Nicky Butt, who would receive the majority of plaudits as an uninspired England made it through to the quarter-finals before succumbing to eventual winners Brazil.

8

The next two seasons saw Liverpool and Gerrard continue to strive for the consistency they needed to challenge Manchester United and Arsenal for the top honours. A win against United in the Worthington Cup final proved that they could live with the best on their day, but their day didn't come round often enough.

For Gerrard, the disappointment of missing out on the World Cup was weighed against the reassurance that his recurring groin injury would be sorted out once and for all through surgery. He continued to be the commanding presence in an ever-changing Liverpool line-up, though his frustration still tended to boil over into red-card aggression from time to time, notably against Chelsea on the final day of the 2002/03 season, when a 2–1 defeat saw the Reds lose out to the Blues in the race for the fourth Champions League spot.

It was enough to convince Roman Abramovich to buy the London club, triggering a spate of unprecedented transfer activity that would drag Gerrard into a web of uncertainty.

Chelsea were back to torment Liverpool on the opening day of the 2003/04 season, with a 2–1 win at Anfield. Two goalless draws followed before the Reds alleviated the pressure on Gérard Houllier with a 3–0 win in the Merseyside derby. That sparked the team into better form, and by the end of the season they had secured the coveted fourth place that qualified them for the Champions League, albeit 30 points behind champions Arsenal, who had gone the entire season unbeaten.

By the summer of 2004, Gerrard had assumed the club captaincy from Sami Hyypia, but, with Chelsea sniffing around, his future at Liverpool looked far from certain. The board had decided to end Houllier's reign and bring in Spaniard Rafa Benitez, while goal-scoring talisman Michael Owen was heading in the other direction, signing for Real Madrid.

There was no time to reflect on such matters, though. For now he had the small matter of his first major international tournament to think about. Sven-Goran Eriksson's impeccable qualification record had seen England through to the European Championships in Portugal, and with a young, talented squad, built around Gerrard and Chelsea's Frank Lampard in central midfield, they fancied their chances.

'I'm flying and the form is good. I'm happy off the pitch. Everything is perfect. I have had a good season,' said Gerrard. 'I think it is well documented that I am not happy with the way it has gone at Liverpool over the past two seasons, but my form has been good.

'I fancy us for the European Championships. I'll be very disappointed if we don't get to the final anyway.'

England met holders France in their opening group game. 'I'm looking at the midfield battle against Vieira, Zidane, Makelele, Pires and Dacourt,' Gerrard exclaimed. 'They are all top class, but I am sure Vieira is saying the same thing about our midfield. We will be right up for it. I am confident we can do really well. We have quality all over the pitch. We have Michael Owen.'

As it turned out, France's midfield overpowered England's, after England had taken the lead through Frank Lampard, and David Beckham had missed the chance to double the advantage from the penalty spot. With France pressing England back into their own penalty area, Zidane curled in a brilliant free-kick to level the scores and then, with only seconds left, Gerrard sold David James dreadfully short with a back pass and the England goalkeeper, lunging for the ball, brought down Thierry Henry for a penalty. Zidane again stepped forward to give France the victory.

And it was another Scouser, 18-year-old Wayne Rooney of Everton, not Michael Owen, who starred for England, as they clawed their way back into the tournament and a quarter-final tie with the hosts, Portugal.

Owen answered his critics by scoring after only three minutes, flicking the ball over Portugal goalkeeper Ricardo after a long kick from David James had evaded the attentions of Costinha. But, after losing Rooney to a broken foot, England again found themselves pinned back into their own half, an ineffective Gerrard was substituted, and almost inevitably Portugal scored a late equaliser. But there was still time for another dramatic twist before extra-time.

Against Argentina in the 1998 World Cup, England had seen an apparently match-winning Sol Campbell header disallowed. Now history repeated itself as Swiss referee Urs Meier disallowed a seemingly legitimate Campbell header right at the end of the match. It would have sent England through. Instead, they had to endure a further 30 minutes of pressure, during which a goal apiece meant the nightmare of penalties once again. And once again England were the losers.

9

Rafa Benitez's first task on assuming the manager's seat at Anfield was to secure the services of Steven Gerrard. Chelsea too had a new manager, and a 'special one', even if Jose Mourinho did say so himself, and, with an apparently limitless transfer budget, the London club was stepping up its pursuit of the Liverpool skipper.

But on 28 June Gerrard allayed Reds fans' fears, announcing that he was staying at Anfield. 'I have gone with the decision that is in my heart,' he said, before adding, 'I have not been happy with the progression at the club over the last two years and, for the first time in my career, I thought about the possibility of moving to another club... but I have decided I am staying on with Liverpool football club and I am 100 per cent committed to them.'

Benitez no doubt breathed a sigh of relief. His second task was to get through qualifying and into the first round of the Champions League, something he achieved courtesy of two goals from his newly committed skipper that gave Liverpool a 2–1 aggregate win against Austrian side AK Graz.

'I've had a few chats with the manager and he told me he wants more goals from midfield,' said Gerrard. 'That's what I'm trying to give him. It's all about me getting forward at the right times and making the right runs.'

Benitez had brought in two fellow countrymen, the classy Xabi Alonso and the tricky Luis Garcia, to bolster Liverpool's creative threat. But Gerrard's goals would be crucial in a season that again saw them stutter in the league, but ended in incredible glory.

In September, Gerrard suffered a double blow at Old Trafford. Liverpool lost 2–1 to arch-rivals Manchester United, and Gerrard left on crutches, having broken the fifth metatarsal in his left foot.

'This is a bad blow for me,' he said. 'I want to be out for as short a time as possible. It was such an innocuous thing. I don't really know how it happened. There was no one near me. I was just stretching to take a pass from Xabi Alonso and my foot stuck in the turf. I heard a crack and it hurt like hell. What is disappointing is that I will miss the Champions League games… It's bad timing.'

In fact, as it turned out, it was good timing. David Beckham had suffered a similar injury which had struck just weeks before the 2002 World Cup, and Wayne Rooney had been forced out of Euro 2004 with the same affliction. But, for Gerrard, there was plenty of time to recover for what would be the high point of his career.

Liverpool's Premiership season stumbled along as if the club itself was struggling to find its feet. They managed to string together more than two consecutive wins only once, and ended up outside the Champions League places, in fifth, behind neighbours Everton.

But they did return to the Millennium Stadium in February for another League Cup final, this time, portentously, against Mourinho's Chelsea. Having rejected the Blues' flirtations in the summer, Gerrard had something to prove as he locked horns with his equally gifted England team-mate Frank Lampard.

Amazingly, John Arne Riise scored inside 45 seconds and Liverpool held that slender lead until one of the most humiliating moments of Gerrard's career. With only 11 minutes remaining, Paolo Ferreira lofted a free-kick into the Reds' penalty area and the captain, jumping higher than Riise and Carragher, inadvertently guided a glancing header into his own net. The first own goal of his professional career left Gerrard visibly distraught. From that moment on, there was only one winner. Chelsea, having dominated the entire match in the face of some dogged Liverpool defending, made the trophy their own with extra-time goals from Didier Drogba and Mateja Kezman. Antonio Nunez made for some last-minute nerves with a late header, but Chelsea held on to their 3–2 lead to lift the Carling Cup.

Gerrard sat slumped on the turf, with tears filling his eyes and the Chelsea fans ironically chanting his name. The Monday-morning newspapers offered little sympathy, with most choosing to acclaim Gerrard's unfortunate own goal as his 'first goal for Chelsea'. For the Liverpool captain, there was no escape from the speculation that his Anfield career was plummeting to its end.

'It was very painful,' grimaced Gerrard after his Cardiff

nightmare. 'Losing any game of football is painful, but to lose a cup final and score an own goal made it a really bad day for me. But I have to be strong, pick myself up and look forward to the next game. We have other things to play for, but that was a tough night.'

And he would have the last laugh over those Chelsea fans. Liverpool's Champions League campaign had stuttered at the group stage, requiring a Gerrard-inspired 3–1 win over Olympiakos at Anfield to see them through. But they had breezed past Bayer Leverkusen then squeezed past Juventus in the knockout rounds to earn a semi-final tie against Mourinho's Premiership-chasing Blues.

A 0–0 draw at Stamford Bridge left the tie perilously in the balance as Chelsea travelled to Anfield for the second leg. Liverpool's defence was under immense pressure not to concede an away goal, but the real drama took place at the other end, where Luis Garcia scored a hotly disputed goal to give Liverpool the win that took them through to their dream Champions League final against AC Milan in Istanbul.

'This is the best night in my life by a million miles,' beamed Gerrard. 'The ground was shaking 50 minutes before the game when we were warming up and I have never known anything like it. At the end I felt like jumping in and celebrating with the fans.'

Following his meteoric rise from Huyton schoolboy to the captain of his beloved football club, the 24-year-old stood poised for the real crowning moment of his career.

Rafa Benitez's gallant heroes were more than equipped with the attributes needed to topple Milan, who had suggested that Liverpool were too defensive and would merely be pushovers.

'We have always been the underdogs and we will be the underdogs in Istanbul,' said Gerrard. 'Everyone thinks Milan will just have to turn up to beat us, but they will be in for a really big fight; we are up for it and we are confident that we will be able to surprise everyone again.'

Did he have a crystal ball?

Liverpool's first poignant victory of the Champions League final came with the news that they would line up in their famous red shirts, with Milan wearing their alternative white strip. It was a good omen considering the fact that when they had played Roma in the 1984 final – the last time they had won the competition – it had been the same colour co-ordination. Indeed, Liverpool had worn red and beaten a team playing in white on each of their four previous European Cup-winning nights.

Five days short of his 25th birthday, Gerrard, having dreamed of the moment for almost all of those 25 years, escorted his team out into the cauldron of noise created by the masses of Liverpool fans convened in the Ataturk Stadium, Istanbul. As the emotion of 'You'll Never Walk Alone' was hollered with all its sincerity from all four corners of the stadium, the Reds captain gathered his team in a huddle to deliver those promised final words of encouragement.

Just over a minute later, and barely 50 seconds into the 50th European Cup final, Milan caught Liverpool off guard as Paolo Maldini, their veteran captain of four winners' medals, swept home Andrea Pirlo's right-wing free-kick. In the blink of an eye, the novelty of the occasion had worn from Liverpool's gaze. Even the most ardent Reds fans feared the worst when Hernan Crespo – on loan to Milan from Chelsea – converted Andriy Shevchenko's low cross to put the Italians two goals ahead. Shevchenko himself had a legitimate goal wrongly disallowed for offside and then, moments before half-time, Crespo impudently finished from Kaka's incisive through-ball to leave Liverpool with a mountain of staggering proportions to climb.

Benitez gathered his players in the small dressing room deep in the bowels of the Ataturk Stadium to deliver the most difficult half-time pep talk of his career. 'I just remember the manager getting his pen out and writing down the changes he wanted on the board,' recalled Gerrard. 'He also said to try and get an early goal as that could make them nervous. But, to be honest, I just couldn't concentrate. There were all sorts of things going through my head; it was weird. I just sat there with my head in my hands. I thought it was over, I really thought it was over.'

Whatever was going through Gerrard's head in that dressing room, it wasn't enough to break his spirit. Soon after the break he started a patient Liverpool attack from the edge of his own penalty area. Just over 20 seconds later, having ghosted forwards unchecked, he rose majestically to loop John Arne Riise's delightful cross from the left into the net. Not renowned for scoring headed goals of such quality – it was only the third of his professional career – Gerrard's goal evoked the magic, the belief that would turn the 2005 Champions League final on its head in six phenomenal minutes.

The captain sprinted back to the halfway line furiously gesturing with his arms, knowing that his side were still in with a chance. Scarcely two minutes later, Vladimir Smicer, making his final appearance for the Reds, took aim from 25 yards and crashed an unstoppable shot into the far corner. Benitez's side had gone from being a beaten team at half-time to being on the verge of an incredible comeback. That revival read complete as Gennaro Gattuso tripped Gerrard inside the penalty area and Xabi Alonso stepped forward to shoulder the enormous responsibility of nudging Liverpool level. The Spaniard saw his effort saved by Dida, but gleefully accepted the rebound to make the score 3–3.

It was simply unbelievable and it seemed to leave everyone in the stadium shell-shocked, including both sets of players. With both teams determined not to yield, the game moved into extra-time. Liverpool's fans fell silent in the second period, as Milan laid siege to the Reds' goal, but found Jerzy Dudek, the Reds' much-maligned goalkeeper, in irrepressible form. Shevchenko powered a downward header against the flailing legs of the Polish custodian and then, incredibly, saw his follow-up somehow turned over the bar. Dudek leaped to his feet nodding his head in disbelief, if not satisfaction. Milan's match-winning chance had gone and penalties ensued – the only way to end such an enthralling game of football.

The Reds' destiny now rested in the lap of the gods – they had not practised penalties in the days leading up to the final. Gerrard, designated as Liverpool's fifth penalty-taker, stood in the middle of a line of bodies – arms linked – on the halfway line. Amid a cacophony of whistling from the Liverpool support, the Brazilian Serginho placed his penalty high over Dudek's crossbar.

Dietmar Hamann was Liverpool's first taker, coolly

slotting his kick to the right of Dida, before the Reds were propelled into dreamland by Milan's crucial second miss. Jerzy Dudek, the hero of the hour, flung himself to his left to deny Andrea Pirlo and then Djibril Cisse put Liverpool two in front. Jon Dahl Tomasson scored for Milan and Liverpool's hearts were forced into overtime again as John Arne Riise saw his effort saved by Dida and then Kaka levelled it at 2–2. But Liverpool had a kick in hand, and Smicer, with his last-ever kick for the Reds, sent Milan's goalkeeper the wrong way.

Shevchenko had to score. Milan's most celebrated player – one of the world's most potent strikers, who had seen his penalty win the competition for Milan two years before – stepped forward and, in what seemed like slow motion, opted to clip his penalty towards the centre of the goal. As Dudek fell to his right, he read Shevchenko's intentions and repelled the ball with his left hand, crowning Liverpool with their fifth European Cup.

Almost every single television camera and photographer courted Gerrard, knowing that it would be his face that painted the best picture of Liverpool's remarkable triumph – never had there been a cup final like it ... anywhere. The Reds' captain embraced everybody in his path as he made his way on a lap of honour to thank the fellow Liverpool fans who had accompanied him on such an amazing, magical journey. Shortly before becoming only the second Scouser after Phil Thompson to lift the European Cup as Liverpool skipper, Gerrard acclaimed the contribution of his manager as he embraced him on the world's television screens.

Talking to ITV, Gerrard pointed to a beaming Benitez,

saying hoarsely, 'We didn't believe we could do it at half-time, but all credit to this man, he never let us put our heads down. We carried on fighting and every one of us deserves credit for that. I'm just made up for the fans: they've saved up for weeks and months to be here – just look at them – 35,000 of them.'

Liverpool's Man of the Match then stepped forward, clasped the trophy in both hands and raised it to the sky. It was, undeniably, the crowning moment of his career to date.

10

With the Champions League trophy locked safely away in the Anfield museum, Liverpool's 2005/06 campaign began with a defiant statement from captain Steven Gerrard, who wanted the Reds to start challenging for the Premiership title.

'It is my responsibility to get this club into the title race. I am the captain, I have committed myself to the club and it is my intention to help us win the title. We are a long way behind and I'm not saying we will do it this year, but we will get closer. I always wanted to stay here and the reason is that I think I can lead Liverpool to the title. I have told the manager he hasn't seen the best of me yet, and I mean that. I am coming to the stage of my career which people say is the prime. Liverpool are going to get the best out of me, and I think I am going to get the best out of Liverpool. Last season we knew that it wasn't good enough. To finish 30 points behind the Premiership winners with a side that won the Champions League is definitely not good enough.'

There was good news from UEFA, who finally decided to allow Liverpool to defend their European crown, but only on the condition that they played three qualifying rounds prior to the group stages of the Champions League. The club began their defence of the trophy with a 3–0 first-round qualifying win over Welsh minnows TNS at Anfield, thanks largely to Gerrard's first-ever professional hat-trick.

A few days before the second leg, Benitez admitted his intention to try to rest his top players during the season in an effort to prevent burnout ahead of the summer's World Cup in Germany.

'We're looking to protect the players, including Stevie. We have been talking about using the whole squad. It's not about using them as much as we can, then just giving them a month to recuperate next summer. It's about selecting the right players for the right games. Sometimes I know we'll make mistakes, but it's my responsibility. At the end of the season I'd hope we've made more right decisions than wrong ones.'

Liverpool fans would have to get used to Benitez's rotation policy, frustrating though it would often prove to be. But Benitez was expecting a long and arduous season. By the time the Premiership campaign started, they had already been playing competitive football for a month, working their way through Champions League qualifying.

On 26 October, they added another trophy to the cabinet, beating UEFA Cup winners CSKA Moscow to bring the European Super Cup to Anfield. Meanwhile, Gerrard was named Most Valuable Player by UEFA for his performance in Istanbul, and the predators were still circling. He was linked with a move to Real Madrid, while a move to champions Chelsea was still deemed to be his most likely chance of ever lifting the Premiership trophy. But Gerrard pledged his allegiance to Liverpool.

'I've been at Anfield since I was eight and it would be wonderful to think I could still be here after hanging up my boots. Whether that would be in a managerial or coaching capacity, I'm not sure, but whatever happens I hope it's linked to Liverpool.'

Further honours followed in the shape of the Ballon d'Or, UEFA's award for Player of the Year, and the PFA Player of the Year award, voted for by his peers in the Premiership. For Liverpool too, it was a much better domestic season than the one before. After a slow start – surprising, given their early season start – they picked up as the season went on, finishing with a run of 10 wins in their last 11 matches – thanks in no small part to the goal-scoring of re-signed Robbie Fowler – to clinch third place, just nine points behind champions Chelsea.

Defence of their European crown fell at the first knockout stage, with a 3–0 aggregate defeat to Benfica, but, as Gerrard had stated at the start of the season, the Premiership was now the priority. Plus, they had beaten Chelsea, that perpetual thorn in Liverpool's side, in the FA Cup semi-final to earn their place in the great showpiece final.

On 23 May 2006, in sweltering heat, Liverpool and West Ham played out one of the most extraordinary FA Cup Finals ever witnessed. West Ham came flying out of the blocks, taking a 2–0 lead through a Carragher own goal and a Dean Ashton strike after a mistake from keeper Pepe Reina.

It was time, once again, for the Steven Gerrard show. Soon after Ashton's goal, Liverpool's French international striker Cisse latched on to an inch-perfect pass from Gerrard to pull the score back to 2–1. Then, 10 minutes after half-time, Gerrard hammered home a rising half-volley from Crouch's knockdown to level the score. Liverpool's delighted fans were rubbing their hands at the prospect of another glorious comeback when they were silenced by a freak goal by West Ham's Paul Konchesky. He sent over a looping cross which deceived Reina and dipped into the far corner of the net to regain the lead for the men from east London.

The Hammers had been the better team, and as the game approached the final whistle, Liverpool fans were beginning to give up the ghost. But with a player like Gerrard in the team there is always hope. And just as the announcement came that there were to be four added minutes, he seized on to a headed clearance to hit possibly his best, and certainly his most dramatic, goal for Liverpool ever. From fully 30 yards, he half-volleyed an incredible strike into the bottom corner of the West Ham net, leaving Shaka Hislop helpless and sending the Liverpool fans into delirium.

After a goalless extra-time, penalties ensued with both sets of players almost dead on their feet. Didi Hamann scored Liverpool's first before Reina saved from Bobby Zamora. Hyypia then saw Hislop save his effort, before 40-year-old Teddy Sheringham brought the Hammers level. Gerrard stood up next and powered his shot into the top right-hand corner. Reina saved from Konchesky, Riise twisted the knife, and then Reina made it a hat-trick of saves by keeping out Anton Ferdinand's kick.

Gerrard lifted the FA Cup as captain for the first time. But for the second time in 12 months, he had left his name indelibly etched on a piece of football history. His career was becoming an endless stream of honours. But now there was an even bigger prize to play for.

Just three weeks later, Gerrard and his England colleagues flew into Baden Baden in the west of Germany to begin their preparations for the World Cup finals. After having missed the 2002 World Cup through injury, Gerrard was eager to make his mark.

'To sit at home bandaged up after groin surgery was probably one of the lowest points of my career,' he confided. 'But I've got a great chance to put that behind me and have a successful tournament.'

He arrived in Germany on the back of one of his most successful seasons ever, having lifted the FA Cup and scored an impressive 23 goals in all competitions. However, he had played in 57 games for Liverpool and England during the season, and it remained to be seen whether he would be able to reproduce his superb club form, especially as England manager Sven-Goran Eriksson still insisted on pairing him with Frank Lampard in the centre of midfield, a combination that had always struggled to gel.

Despite this, many believed that England had their best chance of winning the World Cup since 1966. However, many key players were carrying injuries. Wayne Rooney's partial recovery from another broken metatarsal meant that his debut in the tournament was delayed until the second round. England's other first-choice striker, Michael Owen, had only recently returned to competitive action following a 13-week layoff with his own metatarsal injury.

Before his World Cup debut, against Paraguay in Frankfurt, Gerrard told the BBC, 'Physically, I haven't felt this good my whole career. Mentally, I am fine as well. I have waited a long time for this World Cup to come about and I feel ready for it.'

The team enjoyed a perfect start as captain David Beckham's inswinging free-kick was diverted into Paraguay's net by their own captain, Carlos Gamarra, with just three minutes played. However, as the team wilted in the searing heat, Gerrard dropped into a deeper role in midfield, playing more defensively than he was used to.

Like the majority of England fans, Paraguay midfielder Carlos Paredes said after the match that he felt England were wasting Gerrard's natural talent for getting forward into goal-scoring positions. 'Gerrard is one of the very best midfielders in the world, but in that position, as a defensive holding midfielder, he did not look comfortable. On paper, their midfield should have dominated us. Instead, we dominated them, especially in the second half. Gerrard would have created many more problems for us in his true position.'

The trouble was, it was Lampard's true position too. If they were both to play, one of them had to sit.

The team struggled in its next game against Trinidad and Tobago, who fought gallantly to deny England for three-quarters of the match. Then, with 15 minutes remaining, Crouch rose at the back post to nod home Beckham's deep cross. Gerrard then popped up in the last minute to make the game safe with a wonderful left-foot curler.

England were through to the second round of the World Cup with a game to spare – against Sweden, a country they had failed to beat since 1968. Eriksson made the decision to rest Gerrard, knowing that, as he had already received a booking in the game against Paraguay, a second would rule him out of England's second-round match. Owen Hargreaves took over as defensive midfielder, a role he was far more accustomed to than Gerrard, while Rooney, who had played 30 minutes against Trinidad with no ill effects, started his first match of the tournament in place of Crouch.

However, after just four minutes, the unlucky Michael Owen fell awkwardly and sustained the knee injury which ended his tournament. Nevertheless, England opened the scoring through Chelsea midfielder Joe Cole, who sent the England fans wild with a contender for goal of the tournament when he chested down a headed clearance from a corner and hit a first-time dipping volley. Sweden got back on level terms when Marcus Allback headed home Tobias Linderoth's corner.

With 20 minutes remaining, Eriksson withdrew the tiring Rooney and replaced him with Gerrard, who headed home his second goal of the tournament. But Sweden wouldn't lie down and Henrik Larsson scrambled home a second equaliser in the final minute of the match.

England's prize for winning the group was a match against Ecuador, yet once again the team produced another frustrating display as they limped to a 1–0 victory. Eriksson, trying to find a way to release both Gerrard and Lampard, played five in midfield with Rooney alone up front. But the midfield bursts didn't materialise and it ended up looking like a very defensive formation. It was left to the dead-ball wizardry of Beckham to seal the win and England's passage into the quarter-finals.

Now came a match with Portugal in Gelsenkirchen and a chance to avenge England's Euro 2004 quarter-final defeat. It also pitted Rooney, again playing alone up front, against his Manchester United clubmate Cristiano Ronaldo. But there was no camaraderie on display as Ronaldo proceeded to wind up Rooney, trying to get him in trouble with the referee.

With an hour played, Rooney, who was growing visibly frustrated by the lack of support he was getting up front, appeared to stamp on Ricardo Carvalho following persistent fouling by the Portuguese defender. As the crowd waited for the referee's decision, Ronaldo ran over and gestured to the referee to send Rooney off. The referee duly obliged and England were forced to play the rest of the match with ten men.

To their credit, they kept the score at 0–0 for the remainder of the match, so the outcome, once again, hinged upon a penalty shoot-out. Portugal keeper Ricardo saved penalties from Lampard, Gerrard and his Liverpool team-mate Jamie Carragher. It was left to Ronaldo to apply the coup de grace, sending England out.

Afterwards, Gerrard singled out Ronaldo for his behaviour. After Rooney's dismissal, Ronaldo had turned and winked at his team-mates. 'I saw that,' said Gerrard, 'and if it was one of my team-mates I'd be absolutely disgusted in him because there's no need for that. I've seen Ronaldo going over giving the card and I think he's bang out of order.

'I think that sums him up as a person. If I was playing against my team-mates from Liverpool and they were involved in a situation like that, I'd never try and get them sent off. But we gave everything we could and I hope people don't blame Wayne or the penalty-takers, but if they do we will deal with it.'

The defeat ended the five-year reign of Sven-Goran Eriksson, and Beckham resigned his post as England captain the day after. The weight of opinion suggested Gerrard should inherit the captaincy ahead of his main rival for the post, John Terry. But new England coach Steve McClaren opted for Terry, with Gerrard as vice-captain.

Rafa Benitez saw it as a plus for Liverpool. 'Steven was disappointed, but it's really good for us as he can be fully focused on winning more trophies with Liverpool. He's more mature and a very important player for us as he is our captain. I think he can play for England for another ten years so he will hopefully get another chance to captain his country. I was disappointed for Steven, but Steve McClaren made his decision and I respect that.'

11

Liverpool opened their 2006/07 campaign with a third-round Champions League qualifier at home to Maccabi Haifa, the Israeli champions.

'This game is what you might call the biggest banana skin in football,' said Gerrard ahead of the match. 'We've got to make sure we give a top performance because it would be unthinkable not to get through now.'

However, it was Maccabi who burst out of the blocks more quickly as they took the lead through Gustavo Boccoli, before a debut equaliser from Craig Bellamy just four minutes later and a late curling effort from Gonzalez wrapped up a hard-fought win ahead of the second leg in Israel.

Just four days later, the team travelled to Cardiff to cross swords once more with Premiership champions Chelsea in the Community Shield. The west London club gave debuts to new superstar acquisitions Andriy Shevchenko and Michael Ballack, while Benitez sprang something of a surprise by deciding to rest his captain in anticipation of the Premier League opener at Bramall Lane. He was vindicated by a 2–1 victory.

Liverpool's Premiership campaign got under way with a trip across the Pennines to play newly promoted Sheffield United. With 20 minutes remaining and Liverpool trailing 1–0, Gerrard set off on one of his typical driving runs at the heart of the defence and, after a slick one-two with Fowler, was felled just inside the area by Phil Jagielka. Fowler stepped up to despatch the penalty and earn a share of the spoils.

The penalty was contentious. Gerrard had not actually been tripped by Jagielka, but had fallen while hurdling the defender's outstretched leg. The Liverpool skipper was accused of diving, but Benitez leaped to his defence. 'For me it was a clear penalty. Our player said he felt contact so it was a penalty, simple as that.'

A 2–1 win at home to West Ham was followed by defeats at Everton and Chelsea, as Liverpool continued to struggle for the consistent form that would see them challenge Chelsea and Manchester United for the title. A 2–0 defeat at Old Trafford on 22 October appeared to confirm that they still had some way to go, though they followed it with a 3–1 win at home to Aston Villa, which featured a third goal of the season for new signing Dirk Kuyt.

Three days later, Benitez surprised everyone by naming an unchanged side for the Champions League group game at home to Bordeaux. It was the first time in 100 matches that the Spanish tactician had not rotated his squad and the decision reaped instant rewards as Liverpool romped to a 3–0 victory with two goals from Garcia and one from Gerrard, his first of the season. Liverpool were through to the second round with two games to spare.

But their league form was still wayward. They travelled to Arsenal's brand-new Emirates Stadium looking for a first away win of the season, but it proved to be yet another frustrating away day as Arsenal cantered to a 3–0 win.

In fact, Arsenal would prove to be Liverpool's nemesis that season, knocking them out of both domestic cup competitions in the space of three days in January, both times at Anfield. The League Cup defeat on 9 January was particularly humiliating for Liverpool who, despite goals from Fowler, Gerrard and Hyypia, were thrashed 6–3 by a team of rampaging Arsenal youngsters.

On 6 February, results were overshadowed when, at a specially organised press conference, chief executive Rick Parry introduced George Gillett and Tom Hicks, two American businessmen who had bought control of the club for £174 million. They pledged to bring even more glory and success to the famous old club.

'This is truly the largest sport in the world, the most important sport in the world, and this is the most important club in the most important sport in the world and what a privilege we have to be associated with it,' said Gillett. 'We hope that, with the good graces of Rick and his team, we will be able to enjoy both on-the-pitch success and economic success.

'If you were to put down the list of objectives that Tom and I have, money would be nowhere near the top. It would start with winning; it would start with passion; it would start with respect for tradition and history. It would have the word "legacy" very near the top and it would have the words "thank you to David Moores" for giving us a chance to own this and, hopefully, add to its history.'

Pre-empting concerns among fans unsettled by yet another foreign takeover of an English Premiership club, Hicks added, 'I want to assure the fans that we know what you want. You want to win, I want to win and I know George wants to win.'

But the wins continued to be too infrequent. It was Liverpool's away form that really let them down. They lost nine league games on the road, while a solitary 1–0 defeat to Manchester United was the only blemish on an otherwise unbeaten home record.

Nevertheless, they tightened their grip on third place behind United and Chelsea with a 4–1 win over Arsenal at Anfield, Peter Crouch grabbing a perfect hat-trick. And in the Champions League, things were beginning to snowball once again. Liverpool beat PSV Eindhoven 4–0 on aggregate in the quarter-finals, Gerrard nodding home the first from Finnan's cross to take Ian Rush's crown as Liverpool's top goalscorer ever in the European Cup. It was an achievement that left the Liverpool captain blushing.

'I'm a bit embarrassed to be honest. He is someone I've watched as a kid and I never dreamed I'd break one of his records. I don't think I'll be breaking any of his other ones. I'm flattered, but it's not really important to me. What's more important is how well the team is doing. It was a really good performance and, hopefully, we can go all the way.'

If they were to go all the way, they would have to overcome Chelsea in a repeat of the 2005 semi-final. Before the first leg at Stamford Bridge, Gerrard outlined his determination to reach the final in Athens and have another crack at Europe's biggest prize.

'I want to be remembered as a captain who lifted the trophy twice, or even more. I want to be remembered along with those Liverpool greats like Hughes and Thompson, Souness, Neal and Dalglish. That is why you will see us out there giving it everything tonight, working so hard to give every single ounce of energy we have. Because we want that and we can taste it again.'

Chelsea won the first leg 1–0, but a goal from Danish defender Daniel Agger evened the scored at Anfield and the tie went to penalties. Reina saved from Robben and Geremi to hand Kuyt the chance to clinch the win, which he did with aplomb, sliding his spot kick into the bottom corner.

Amazingly, a second Champions League final in two years was inked into Reds fans' diaries, and, just as before, they would be facing AC Milan in the final. But the disappointing statistic for everyone was that the club had finished 21 points behind champions Manchester United. They had finished only nine points behind Chelsea the season before, and the quest for domestic supremacy had taken a backwards step.

Nevertheless, a trip to Athens beckoned and with it a chance for the club to pick up a major piece of silverware for the third year in a row. Just as in Istanbul two years previously, Liverpool took a massive following with them to Athens. UEFA came under heavy criticism from the club for their decision to grant only 17,000 tickets to each club in a ground built to hold 63,000 people. Ridiculously, UEFA had allocated 20,000 of the seats in the stadium to corporate guests, with the other 10,000 being sold via a general ballot on the UEFA website.

The day and night before the final, the main square in the

city, Syntagma Square, was awash with Liverpool fans, with figures estimated to be in the region of 40,000–45,000. Gerrard spoke of the team's determination to go out and win 'Ole Big Ears' for a second time in three seasons.

'We've come on so much as a team and don't see reaching this stage as a bonus any more. I'd go further and say I actually expected us to be challenging to win it. What we've done so far is fantastic, but it's not a surprise to us. Going on to win is what matters.'

On the day of the game, Benitez, always likely to throw a surprise in his team selections, chose to start with just one striker, Kuyt, with Gerrard behind him as an auxiliary striker. Crouch was named on the bench. The logic behind Benitez's thinking was to allow him to field Alonso and Mascherano in the centre of midfield, with the Argentine assigned the task of keeping the ever-dangerous Kaka quiet.

As the teams came out on to the pitch, with Liverpool again wearing their famous all-red kit and Milan in all-white, the volume around the ground proved deafening. Huge roars greeted the names of the starting XI for Liverpool before the vociferous singing of Liverpool's anthem, 'You'll Never Walk Alone', preceded kick-off.

The first real chance of the final fell to Jermaine Pennant, but his cross-shot was pushed away by Dida in the Milan goal, before Xabi Alonso flashed a low shot just wide of the post. After enjoying a lot of possession in the first half, Liverpool were desperately unlucky to go in at half-time 1–0 down, after a free-kick from Andrea Pirlo deflected off Filippo Inzaghi and into the net with Reina stranded.

The second half witnessed Gerrard trying to inspire his team back into the game. First Dida blocked his run and low shot, before his attempt from long range zipped just wide. Then, with ten minutes of the final remaining, Kaka, whose shadow Mascherano had by now been replaced as Liverpool searched for an equaliser, slipped in a slide-rule pass to Inzaghi who rounded Reina to put Milan 2–0 up. A late Kuyt header gave Liverpool fresh belief that they could find an equaliser, but, unlike in Istanbul, 2007 was to be Milan's year.

News only filtered through the next day that roughly 2,000 Liverpool fans holding authentic tickets had been refused entry to the Olympic Stadium for the final. Police said the reason was that the ground was already full. Another fine mess caused by UEFA.

Gerrard revealed his total devastation at the result. 'You've got to take it on the chin, move on and try to pick yourself up, but at the moment it's heartbreaking. I thought we started well, we were in control just how we like to be, but when you do that you've got to score. They got the first goal with a bit of luck, but it was a big lift for them. We gave everything, but it wasn't to be tonight and certainly this feels the complete opposite to what it was like after Istanbul.'

And, after a trophyless season, he remained focused on the future and the quest for the Premiership.

'Winning the league next season has got to be a priority for me, the manager, the players and the new people in charge. It's been a long time since this club won the league and we have to improve in the Premiership and give it a better go.

'Since the takeover happened, you can feel the optimism, you can feel the fans' excitement, and the players and staff are no different – we are all looking to the future with great optimism. This team will be strengthened and then it's down to the players to perform and earn the right to be title contenders. The fans have been hugely supportive but now it's time for us to deliver.'

Gerrard did have reason to celebrate before the start of the new season, when he married his fiancée Alex Curran, the mother of his daughters Lilly-Ella and Lexie, on 16 June 2007 at Cliveden in Buckinghamshire. It must have been something in the stars: his England colleagues Gary Neville and Michael Carrick also got married on the same day.

Benitez had his own match-making mission to take on as he began work on trying to create a team capable of challenging for the 2007/08 Premiership title by persuading Carragher, Reina, Alonso and Sissoko to sign new long-term deals. Meanwhile, at the start of July, he announced the exciting arrival of Spanish striker Fernando Torres. The signing cost the club a record £27 million and was an indication that the Americans were serious about putting on-the-pitch results at the top of their list of priorities.

Torres scored his first league goal in a 1–1 home draw with Chelsea and quickly struck up a rapport with Gerrard that had the Reds firing on all cylinders. They were unbeaten in the league going into December, with both men regularly among the goals, and there was serious talk that this might just be the year Liverpool won the title for the first time since 1990. They were keeping clean sheets too, the latest a 4–0 thrashing of Bolton that saw Torres and Gerrard on the scoresheet.

Next up was a home game against Reading, but the Berkshire side, ably managed by Steve Coppell, recorded a shock 3–1 at Anfield that rattled the Reds for the first time. They were still wobbling a week later when champions Manchester United beat them 1–0 at Old Trafford, and then Chelsea knocked them out of the League Cup with a 2–0 quarter-final defeat at Stamford Bridge.

Things were altogether better in the Champions League, where they had rallied after consecutive defeats to Marseille and Besiktas in October to finish the group with three straight wins, including an 8–0 demolition of Besiktas at Anfield that featured a hat-trick from new playmaker Yossi Benayoun, signed from West Ham.

But a winless January saw Liverpool loosen their grip on the Premiership, and, although they lost only one more game from the start of February – a 3–0 defeat to eventual champions Manchester United at Old Trafford – too many draws and their failure to beat any of the other top four sides meant they had to settle for fourth place in an exciting end to the season that saw United, Chelsea and Arsenal finish within four points of each other, seven points clear of Benitez's side.

Liverpool did manage to beat Arsenal in the Champions League quarter-final, with Gerrard and Torres both among the goals again, along with Hyypia and Babel, in a decisive 4–2 second-leg victory at Anfield. And, with United, Liverpool and Chelsea all making it through to the semi-finals, along with Barcelona, fate paired them with Chelsea for yet another epic semi-final.

Jose Mourinho's 'special' reign at Stamford Bridge had come to an end and he had been replaced by Avram Grant.

Kuyt scored for Liverpool in a 1–1 first-leg draw at Anfield, leaving Liverpool in need of an away goal at the very least at Stamford Bridge. Didier Drogba gave Chelsea the lead after half an hour, but Torres hit back after 63 minutes to level the tie, away goals and all.

The game slipped into extra-time and Liverpool started well, Hyypia heading narrowly wide from a corner. When a Michael Essien goal for Chelsea was ruled out for offside, it looked like it could be Liverpool's night, but two minutes later their luck ran out. Michael Ballack, bursting into the Liverpool box, was brought down by Hyypia and the ref pointed to the spot. Up stepped Frank Lampard, recovering from the death of his mother the week before, to plant the penalty past Reina and celebrate with a poignant look to the heavens.

Even so, Chelsea were by no means home and dry. One goal for Liverpool would be enough to take them through on the away-goals rule. And in Torres they had a striker who could conjure a goal out of nothing. So Liverpool fans were understandably bewildered when Benitez took Torres off and replaced him with Babel.

Chelsea, buoyed by Lampard's goal, took the initiative and Drogba extended their lead after a run and cross from Liverpool old boy Nicolas Anelka. Now the Reds had a mountain to climb, and, though Babel pulled one back with four minutes of extra-time remaining, it was too little too late. Chelsea had taken their revenge and would go on to meet Manchester United in the first-ever all-English Champions League final.

Liverpool fans, Steven Gerrard among them, could only look for ways of avoiding their TV sets as United, their fiercest rivals from up the East Lancs Road, triumphed over Chelsea in Moscow, completing a League and European Double that had once been the exclusive property of Liverpool Football Club.

12

When Alex Ferguson became manager of Manchester United, way back in 1986, his first priority had been to break the dominance of Liverpool. It had taken him a while, but, since clinching the first Premiership title in 1993, United had become the undoubted kings of English football, winning 11 Premier League titles in 16 years.

Now Rafa Benitez had to perform the same feat in reverse. If Liverpool were to fulfil Steven Gerrard's dream of becoming English champions, they would have to match the hunger and consistency that Ferguson had instilled at Old Trafford. Ferguson had declared his admiration for Gerrard on more than one occasion – indeed, he had regarded him as the ideal replacement for Roy Keane – but the two had never had the pleasure of working together.

In fact, that would have been unthinkable. Not many players move between Liverpool and United, and, if Gerrard couldn't get excited about lifting the Premiership trophy in a Chelsea shirt, the thought of doing so in a United shirt must have left him cold.

And so, when Liverpool beat United 2–1 at Anfield in their fourth match of the 2008/09 campaign, and swiftly followed that win with five straight victories that took them to November unbeaten, he must have sensed that his decision to stay loyal to Liverpool could soon be vindicated.

Benitez had been criticised for his constant squad rotation, in particular his tendency to rest Gerrard and Torres just as they were building up a head of steam, but now his tactics appeared to be paying off. A 2–1 defeat at Tottenham on 1 November was followed by another unbeaten run that lasted until 28 February, when Middlesbrough recorded a 2–0 at the Riverside.

During Mourinho's reign at Chelsea, the Portuguese manager had been a constant tormentor of his Spanish counterpart, Benitez seemingly helpless to resist being drawn into distracting wars of words that tended to backfire on him. Now, with Mourinho gone, it fell to Ferguson to dangle the bait for Benitez. And how he bit.

Ferguson had complained about the fixture calendar, hinting that the football authorities might have handed Liverpool an advantage, and adding that nerves might scupper Liverpool's endeavours in building on their strong first half of the season to secure the title.

Benitez exploded. Reading from a script, he stunned a press conference by directing a rant at the Manchester United manager.

'I was surprised by what has been said,' he began, 'but maybe they are nervous because we are at the top of the table.' He then said he wanted to talk about facts, and referred to his prepared paper.

'I want to be clear, I do not want to play mind games too early, although they seem to want to start. But I have seen some facts. On 1 November, they played Hull and Mr Ferguson had a two-match touchline ban and a £10,000 fine after confronting Mike Dean, the referee, for improper conduct.'

Benitez then cited instances where United had benefited from questionable refereeing decisions, and implied that Ferguson appeared to be the one getting special treatment from the powers that be.

'During the Respect campaign – and this is a fact – Mr Ferguson was charged by the FA for improper conduct after comments made about Martin Atkinson and Keith Hackett. He was not punished. He is the only manager in the league that cannot be punished for these things.

'Then he was talking about the fixtures. Two years ago we were playing a lot of early kick-offs away on Saturdays when United were playing on Sundays. And we didn't say anything. Now he is complaining about everything, that everybody is against United. But the second half of the season will see them playing at home against all the teams at the top of the table. It is a fantastic advantage.

'I am not playing mind games, just facts,' he repeated, before adding mischievously, 'If he wants to talk about fixtures, and have a level playing field as you say in England, there are two options if we don't want more problems with fixtures. One is the same as in Spain, the draw for the first part of the league is known, everyone knows which weekend. In the second half everyone plays the opposite, so you all know. Sky and Setanta have the right to choose their games and it will be the same for everyone. So Mr Ferguson will not be complaining about fixtures and a campaign against United.

'Or there is another option: that Mr Ferguson organises the fixtures in his office and sends it to us and everyone will know and cannot complain. That is simple.'

Benitez was on a roll, and he took the opportunity to lob a few provocative remarks back in the direction of United.

'Are they under pressure? Maybe they were not thinking that we would be at the top of the table in January. But we are at the top of the table and they are nervous.

'I am not telling the authorities what to do. But I have been here for five years and know how things are going on. I will be watching United's game with Chelsea. The result does not matter to us, if we win at Stoke that result does not matter.'

The gathered reporters were gobsmacked. Why had Benitez decided to choose this moment, with Liverpool sitting on top of the table and United about to face a difficult game against Chelsea, to swallow Ferguson's bait? Benitez offered his explanation.

'I have decided that I had a lot of information and I have been watching every single week what has been going on. Then they started talking about us, but every single week we know they will be talking. But we want to stay at the top and maybe they will talk about us right to the end.

'To hear someone talking when he has problems with referees every single week, and now complaining about the fixtures and complaining about everything, I think that is not fair.'

To many observers, Benitez was telling some home truths that were long overdue. But in terms of his personal duel with Ferguson – a duel that could have a major bearing on the title race – he appeared to have blinked first, lost his cool and handed a tremendous moral victory to the United man.

It certainly looked that way when a rampant United hammered Chelsea 3–0 and Liverpool were then held to a 0–0 draw at Stoke. Two 1–1 draws followed, at home to Everton and away to Wigan, and by the time the Reds got back to winning ways with a 2–0 win over Chelsea, thanks to two late Torres strikes, United had moved into top spot – a position they would hold until the end of the season.

Liverpool finished strongly to claim second place, their best position since 2002, and their best points total with 86. But still the title eluded them, and, whether Benitez had blown it or not with his decision to lock horns with Ferguson while sitting pretty at the top in January, it was another season gone by for Steven Gerrard without winning the prize he wanted more than any other.

It was a second season on the trot without a trophy for the Reds, knocked out of the FA Cup by Everton in a replay at Goodison, beaten by Spurs in the fourth round of the League Cup, and falling foul of Chelsea in their customary Champions League showdown, this time in the quarter-finals. Trailing 3–1 from the home leg, they went to Stamford Bridge without Gerrard, sidelined through injury, and gave it all they'd got in a thrilling 4–4 draw. Having taken a 2–0 lead after 20 minutes, it looked like they might turn the tie around, but Chelsea rallied after the break, and, once they'd equalised on the night through a fierce free-kick from Alex, Liverpool were playing for pride.

Once again, the inspirational captain had had a brilliant season. He was the league's third top goalscorer with 16, two ahead of Torres, and he was voted Footballer of the Year by the Football Writers' Association. But injuries and Benitez's rotation policy had meant that neither he nor Torres had played as many games as the Kop faithful would have liked, and without their deadly duo Liverpool just didn't look the same.

It is a mark of Gerrard's character and talent as a footballer that he has spent his career winning plaudits and honours in a side in continual transition, sometimes threatening to challenge the top sides, but never quite making the grade and falling away again. His determination has driven his beloved Liverpool to achieve great things: the Champions League triumph in Istanbul and the FA Cup final win against West Ham are both memorable for the way Gerrard stepped forward from the ranks of his flagging team-mates and turned the tide in Liverpool's favour.

Sure, he has had his allies along the way. Michael Owen, Gary McAllister, Didi Hamann, Jamie Carragher, Xabi Alonso and most recently Fernando Torres have all played complementary roles to Gerrard's burgeoning presence. But, without him, who knows what Liverpool would have achieved in the last decade?

The 2009/10 season has seen Liverpool slip back again in their pursuit of Premier League glory. With Tottenham,

Aston Villa and big-spending Manchester City all staking valid claims for a Champions League berth, the target for the season soon had to be lowered from first place to fourth – an outcome guaranteed by Benitez but by no means a foregone conclusion.

With early exits from both domestic cups and slipping out of the Champions League into the Europa League, rumours started to circulate once more that Gerrard might be contemplating a move away from Anfield. There was talk of a dressing-room bust-up between him and Benitez at half-time in the shock FA Cup exit at home to Reading. But Gerrard dismissed the rumours as 'fantasy'.

'I've heard about a dozen versions of the same rumour and they're all as daft as each other,' he said. 'I'd love to know who comes up with this kind of stuff because they must have an unbelievable imagination. Nothing happened, that's an absolute fact. And if anyone thinks this nonsense unsettles either me or the club then they're mistaken. If anything it's brought everyone even closer together because we've all had a good laugh about it.

'In the time since he's been here, I've never had a problem with the manager or his staff, and certainly not at half-time in the Reading game, when I was actually receiving treatment for the injury I'd picked up during the first half.'

Such speculation will always follow a player of the quality of Steven Gerrard. Whether or not Liverpool win the Premiership, other clubs will always covet his services. But with over 500 appearances to his name, and a goal-scoring record of one in four, his contribution to Liverpool has been nothing short of immense. The Bambi who became a bison has already ensured his place in Anfield history several times over.

His puffed-out chest has become an icon for the club, decorated with the medals of his thrilling cup endeavours. And there's still room for more, starting with a World Cup winners' medal this summer.